the WORDS *of*
JUSTICE
BRANDEIS

the WORDS *of* JUSTICE BRANDEIS

edited by SOLOMON GOLDMAN

with a Foreword by
JUSTICE WILLIAM O. DOUGLAS

 HENRY SCHUMAN · NEW YORK

to

DAVID JACKER

in admiration, gratitude, and deep affection

CONTENTS

vii

*

FOREWORD

There are some who identify themselves with a cause and then use it to advance their own interests. There are others who lose themselves in the cause, staking their reputations, their fortunes, and their lives that it may live. Government, business, labor, the professions, science, literature and the arts have had men and women of both types. But the person who has made some cause greater than himself is still so rare as to deserve a special tribute.

There was a letter written to the late George W. Norris, reminding him that if he cast his vote for a certain measure before the Senate, he would never represent the people of Nebraska again. His reply was the measure of the man—that the important thing was not his own political survival but the survival of the idea embodied in the controversial measure.

That attitude also marked the man Brandeis. His obsession was with causes—Zionism, honesty in government, integrity in business and finance, the curse of bigness in our economic and political life. Much of his advocacy exposed him to scorn and to the bitterness of powerful opposition. The enemies he made almost defeated his confirmation as Associate Justice of the Supreme Court. But, knowing Brandeis, I know there was no price he would not have paid for his convictions. Causes were not lost in the man; he was dedicated to his causes.

That is why the words he spoke, the advice he gave, the positions he defended will always be worth review and study. Some of his phrases could have been turned into more colorful literature by a Holmes. But no one could have improved on the power of his logic. And the fire of his convictions transformed simple words into the statement of fighting faiths.

Rabbi Solomon Goldman has done a scholarly job in culling out from voluminous material many enduring ideas with which Brandeis was associated and numerous statements of a philosophy of life adaptable to the vicissitudes of a changing century. These utterances of Brandeis will stir warm and vibrant memories in all those who knew the man. To those who never had that privilege this collection will give some clues to his greatness.

William O. Douglas

WASHINGTON, D.C.
MAY 17, 1952.

*

PREFACE

Between July 1938 and September 1941 I had the privilege
of seeing Justice Brandeis as many as forty-five times. He
would receive me as a rule at eight in the morning and the
conversation would last a full hour. I also attended, during
that period, several conferences at the Brandeis home, and
was present at the only meeting which took place between
the Justice and the late Dr. Chaim Weizmann after the
breach between the two in 1920. Prior to 1938 I listened to
Mr. Brandeis at several Zionist meetings, spent two hours in
his company July 4, 1921, at a Pittsburgh hotel, as a member of the committee that formulated the resolution calling into existence the Palestine Development Council, and
talked with him in Washington and Chatham in 1924,
1926, 1928, 1932, 1936, and 1937.

The first time I saw and heard Mr. Brandeis on a public
platform was in 1913. When I heard him again in 1914 for
the second time I was so moved by the very conciseness of

his remarks that I went rummaging in New York's libraries for more of his words. My search was soon rewarded. For it led me to his then recently published *Business—A Profession*. The reading of this book was a new experience for me. For it opened up worlds of which I had as little knowledge as of the Milky Way. Not that I had not known that they were there, but I thought of them as curios. *Business—A Profession* made me realize to what extent I was implicated in those new worlds.

From that time on I read everything written by or about Mr. Brandeis that did not escape my attention and on which I could lay my hands. Following an early reading habit, I marked in the books, pamphlets, and articles I was reading passages coming under the following four categories: general ideas, whether original in essence or only in form and application; elucidations and affirmations of American principles; similarities between Americanism and Judaism; and echoes from the Bible, whether of its content or style. In 1933 I read avidly Professor Alpheus Thomas Mason's *Brandeis: Lawyer and Judge in the Modern State*. From then on I looked forward eagerly to whatever came from the pen of that most brilliant and consecrated of the biographers of Justice Brandeis.

By the time I began to see the Justice frequently I had accumulated an abundance of Brandeisiana, which was soon supplemented by the views he expressed in the conversations I had with him. The desire to make use of all this material was irrepressible. Unfortunately, I never got to write more than a few pieces, three of which appeared in *The New Palestine* and one each in *The Jewish Frontier* and the Israeli *Gilyonot*. For Time, ever niggardly with modern clergymen, had in store for me other plans and trials and a freak accident that have imposed restrictions on my literary interests.

May the reader, if there should ever be one to glance at

this Preface, forgive me for writing in so personal a vein. I do so both to explain what it was that impelled me to compile this little volume and to apologize for publishing it in its present state of incompleteness and imperfection. Let him bear with me. I come only, belatedly, to pay homage to the memory of one of the greatest men of our times for having afforded me the privilege of sitting at his feet.

Now as to the sources to which I am indebted. Mr. Brandeis, it should be noted, was not a professional writer or scholar. That is, his primary aim was not to produce books. He was one of those rare social philosophers who was far more interested in the day-to-day improvement of the present than in envisaging Utopian futures. Furthermore, the writing of a continuous book, setting forth a philosophical system, he most probably regarded as too "big" and presumptuous an undertaking for a mortal man. He deemed it sufficient to treat of one specific, concrete problem at a time, and he wrote and spoke only to help in the solution of the problem before him. Consequently his "literary" activity took the form of addresses, lectures, articles, pamphlets, discussions, statements, and cross-examinations before a variety of government and citizens' commissions, interviews, briefs, opinions, and letters.

Of this material Small, Maynard & Company published, in 1914 and again in 1925, under Mr. Brandeis' name *Business—A Profession*. Both editions contain a chapter on Mr. Brandeis by Ernest Poole which was first published in the *American Magazine* in February, 1911. The 1925 edition contains Supplementary Notes by Mr. Justice Felix Frankfurter. (Professor Mason does not mention this second edition but instead an edition of 1933, published by Hale, Cushman & Flint, which edition I have not seen.) Also in 1914 F. A. Stokes & Company issued, and in 1932 the National Home Library Foundation reissued, also under the name of the Justice, and with a Preface by Norman

Hapgood, *Other People's Money and How the Bankers Use It*. Two earlier books bearing the Justice's name were privately printed in 1894–96 and 1907. (These books I have never seen, and know only from references to them in Professor Mason's works on Justice Brandeis.)

In addition to these two books there further appeared selections and extracts from the Justice's papers in the following works:

De Haas, Jacob. *Louis D. Brandeis: A Biographical Sketch*. Bloch Publishing Co., New York, 1929. The volume contains the "full text of his [Brandeis'] Addresses [on Zionism]" delivered from 1912 to 1924.

Flexner, Bernard. *Mr. Justice Brandeis and the University of Louisville*. Privately printed by the University of Louisville in 1938.

Fraenkel, Osmond K., Editor. *The Curse of Bigness*. The Viking Press, New York, 1934.

Goldman, Solomon, Editor. *Brandeis on Zionism*. Prepared for publication by Abraham G. Duker and Carl Alpert and published by the Zionist Organization of America with an Introductory Note by Judge Louis E. Levinthal and a Foreword by Justice Frankfurter. Washington, D.C., 1942.

Lief, Alfred, Editor. *The Social and Economic Views of Mr. Justice Brandeis*. Published by the Vanguard Press with a Foreword by Professor Charles A. Beard. New York, 1934. (Mr. Lief's *The Brandeis Guide to the Modern World*, published by Little, Brown & Co., Boston, 1941, did not come to my attention until after this volume was completed. While our compilations are unavoidably similar in some respects, they diverge sufficiently not to render, I hope, my effort superfluous.)

Lives of and Tributes to the Justice and expositions of his views that I have read include among others the following:

Analyticus [James Waterman Wise]. *Jews Are Like That!* Brentano's, New York, 1928.

De Haas. Listed above.

Frankfurter, Felix, Editor. *Mr. Justice Brandeis.* Yale University Press, with an Introduction by Justice Holmes. New Haven, 1932.

Goodhart, Arthur L. *Five Jewish Lawyers of the Common Law.* Oxford University Press, London–New York–Toronto, 1949.

Jackson, Justice Robert H. "Louis D. Brandeis." *The Jewish Frontier*, July, 1943.

Levinthal, Louis E. "Louis Dembitz Brandeis." *American Jewish Year Book*, 1942–43.

Lief, Alfred. *Brandeis: The Personal History of an American Ideal.* Stackpole Sons, New York–Harrisburg, Pa., 1936.

Mason, Alpheus Thomas. *Brandeis: Lawyer and Judge in the Modern State.* Princeton University Press, Princeton, 1933. Republished in 1936 with a Foreword by Norman Hapgood by the National Home Library

Foundation under the abbreviated title *Brandeis and the Modern State.*

—*The Brandeis Way: A Case Study in the Workings of Democracy.* Princeton University Press, Princeton, 1938.

—*Bureaucracy Convicts Itself: The Ballinger-Pinchot Controversy of 1910.* The Viking Press, New York, 1941.

—*Brandeis: A Free Man's Life.* The Viking Press, New York, 1946.

Harvard Theological Review, December, 1941.

Opinion, A Journal of Jewish Life and Letters. November, 1941.

Proceedings of the Bar of the Supreme Court of the United States and Meeting of the Court in Memory of Associate Justice Louis D. Brandeis, December 21, 1942. Published in Washington, 1942.

The New Palestine, November, 1941.

All of the above Lives contain copious extracts from the oral and written words of Justice Brandeis. All of them put me under obligation, more particularly so Professor Mason and his *A Free Man's Life,* in which he gives numerous quotations from the Justice's unpublished letters.

I am indebted to the Justice himself for the material to be found in this volume under the following headings: Abstract Thinking, A Day's Work, Amendment, American Jewish Community, Angels and Devils, Anti-Semitism and the Nazis, Bible, Chosen People, Benjamin V. Cohen, William O. Douglas, God's Presence, God's Purpose, History, Immortality of the Soul, Jewish Festivals, Joiners,

Messiah, Miracles, Neutrality, Practical Men, Punctuality, Radicals and Conservatives, Resurrection, Revelation, Theodore Roosevelt and Woodrow Wilson, Sabbath, Scientists and Theologians, Specialization, Unwieldy Committees, White Paper on Palestine, and Zionism. Ever so often during my visits to the Brandeis home, when the business that brought me there was at an end and the hour the Justice put at my disposal had not yet run out, he would allow me to draw him into a discussion of various Jewish and religious problems that I knew he had not dealt with elsewhere. I never took notes in his presence but made it a practice to record what he had said at the earliest possible opportunity. I am confident that I have reproduced his views faithfully, and perhaps also his language if my memory has not played me false.

The piece entitled American and Jew immediately following consists of excerpts from articles I previously published and of which I have made mention above.

It remains only for me to express my deep gratitude to the ever faithful and competent Mrs. Henry Baum for preparing the manuscript.

Solomon Goldman

VERNON TOWNSHIP
FEBRUARY 17, 1952

PART ONE

JUSTICE BRANDEIS— AMERICAN AND JEW

*

Those who enjoyed the privilege of seeing Justice Brandeis at close range could not fail to be struck by the spontaneous, contagious optimism of the man. It was not a mood; it was not stimulated by the urgency of causes or evoked by the despair of their advocates. His optimism flowed from the inner being of the man.

I was never more impressed with it than when, in 1938, I came to the Brandeis home with one of the country's eminent citizens, a religious leader of high repute, Mr. Brandeis' junior by several years. The man leaned heavily on a cane. His old age trod falteringly. He relaxed into his chair hopelessly, and soon began to expostulate on the evils of the times and to moan in sheer helplessness against the dark impasse of our civilization.

"I cannot agree with you," interjected Justice Brandeis, and the words sounded natural—"I cannot agree with you. We are moving on. There is much to be done, of course, but

· 3

I am very optimistic. What we need . . ." Here the Justice
spoke concisely, logically, almost mathematically, of what
might be done in the United States and elsewhere to
fashion the shape of things to come. I thought of the
tribute paid him on the occasion of his seventy-fifth birthday by the man who knew him better than most men.
Justice Holmes then wrote: "In the moments of discouragement that we all pass through, he always has had the happy
word that lifts up one's heart. . . ."

*

There was in Justice Brandeis that elusive something
which set him apart, which made men hold their breath
when in his presence. For here was a realist, ruthless arith-
metician, stubborn analyst, and scientific materialist who
dealt all his life with business, money, unions, trusts, and
monopolies, and who, in all his adult life, had never come
under the direct influence of religion, who may perhaps be
best described as a saint. Here was a Jew who was reared
with little knowledge of his people, who rarely felt the sting
of anti-Semitism, who, as a youth, was accepted by the best
families of blue-blooded Boston, who yet became the most
optimistic and enthusiastic Zionist on this side of the
Atlantic. Somewhere in the unriddling of this paradox will
be found the essence of Mr. Brandeis' being, the quality
of his personality.

*

The passion for freedom, some of Mr. Brandeis' biographers suggest, is in the Brandeis blood. Unfortunately,
they limit it to the immediate family. They record the fact
that his maternal grandfather participated in the Polish
uprising of 1830 and that his father and uncle, Lewis Dembitz, though Southerners, were on the side of the Union.
The biographers have forgotten a verse in Leviticus reading
—"And ye shall proclaim liberty unto all the inhabitants

thereof." They have overlooked numerous chapters in Isaiah and the Psalms, as well as the whole of the prolonged and glorious struggle for freedom of conscience of the people from which Mr. Brandeis sprang. It is not amiss to point out, when speaking of Mr. Brandeis, that the one little people in antiquity that bled for its freedom with abandon and for two centuries fought undaunted one of the most powerful military machines the world had ever known, was the Jewish people. Statues of Roman emperors, symbol of Roman superstition, autocracy and dictatorship, were worshiped the world over, but not in Judea.

*

Though the home of young Brandeis' parents had lost contact with the Jewish world, it was not wanting in echoes and reminiscences of Jewish tragedy, grandeur, and aspiration. Long before the Justice, members of his family dreamed Messianic dreams and envisioned prophetic Utopias. There were Brandeises who had been martyred for the faith and Dembitzes who had followed the dead-end trails blazed by Sabbatai Zevi and Jacob Frank. Young Brandeis listened with rapt excitement to the wondrous legends of Rabbi Loewe, a distant ancestor of the family, and tales of grief, hope, and disillusionment which his Uncle Lewis would tell. He did not understand all he heard. The *mise en scène* was strange, the figures exotic, the action mysterious, but there remained in the subconscious vague recollections of Jews anxious for freedom and waiting for a Messiah. It is not improbable that these recollections occasionally streamed into the consciousness of the maturing Brandeis.

Mr. Brandeis' mother, daughter of a Polish rebel, and descendant of men who preserved their dignity and individuality against the cruelty and violence of princes and counts, carried food and coffee to an encampment of

Northern soldiers. That she took young Louis with her
was only in consonance with a tradition bidding Jewish
parents habituate their young in the practice of *mitzvot,*
"good deeds." "Train up a child in the way he should go:
and when he is old he will not depart from it."

The mother gave the boy who trudged along at her side
a good training in the *mitzvah* and value of freedom. Often
Louis asked numerous questions: What were the soldiers
doing at the encampment? What were they fighting for?
Why did people want slaves? Why were some people's
skins black? Did black skins protect people against suffering pain? Could a black skin bleed? Did being black outside also mean being black on the inside? Could a black boy
learn to read and write? Does a black boy love his mother?
Do black boys like to play? Why did you, Mama and
Papa and Uncle Lewis Dembitz, leave Europe and come
here? Were there no houses there? What was Grandpa
like? I wonder whether anybody brought him coffee and
food when he was a soldier.

Young Louis was stimulated as he tried to understand
the answers that came from the patient, kind lips of his
mother. The tall, slender lad sometimes lingered behind
meditating and sometimes rushed ahead impatiently. He
walked, mused, and whistled as if his young heart and mind
were unable to contain all that his mother had told him, as
if the future people's attorney was chafing to do something
about it all.[1]

It was good he was whistling, for this whistling saved
him for the great struggle for freedom and democracy to
which his life was to be dedicated. When he was but a youth,

---

[1] This account of mother and son is not imaginary. That the boy
Louis occasionally accompanied his mother on her hazardous
missions I learned from Mrs. Brandeis; that the Justice was moved
by this account of his mother and himself, when he first read it in
The New Palestine, I heard from one of his cousins in Washington.

his parents sent him to Dresden, Germany, to continue his education there. (Americans for a long time—
even the liberty-loving "Forty-Eighters"—deferred to Germany in matters educational.) One evening young Brandeis, while a student in a Dresden school, forgot the key
to his room, and upon his return to the dormitory, whistled
to arouse his roommate. On the morrow he was severely
disciplined. Mr. Brandeis informed his parents that he had
had enough of Kultur. "This made me sick," he reported
many years later. "In Kentucky you could whistle. . . ."

*

His native gifts, his uncanny grasp of figures, his easy
penetration into the intricacies of big business, his unflag-
ging capacity for work, his meticulous orderliness, his
magnetic personality, brought him a large and lucrative
clientele. The wealthiest corporations, the most affluent
citizens, sought as their lawyer this tall Lincolnesque
Kentuckian who was sure to win their cases. After a
decade or more, Mr. Brandeis was confronted with the need
of making a difficult decision. He was coming into wealth.
He was moving in the circles of the mighty. He was a
welcome guest in the most elegant parlors, where affluence
and affability were the most prized of virtues. He saw himself drawn into a circle where desire was fanned and the
spirit restrained, license encouraged and liberty diluted.
Things were preferred to ideas, money to men, and power
to character. Mr. Brandeis discovered that it was embar-
rassing to whistle. There was no Junker *Schutzmann* to
stop or punish him, but it was just not being done in the
elegant parlors of Boston.

He was ill at ease. There were the wistful tales of mother
on those lonely marches to the encampment of soldiers;
there were the challenging utterances of the aged Emerson,
whom he had heard as a student. There was the Puritan

heritage, there was the intimate knowledge of the Constitution, of the Declaration of Independence, and there were
some vague recollections of stories Uncle Dembitz had told
about the Maccabees. And Mr. Brandeis decided: "I have
only one life to live and it is short enough. Why waste it
on things that I don't want most? And I don't want money
or property most. I want to be free. It is not only tyrants
who enslave men; property, money and things can become
the implacable foes and thieves of freedom. Freedom sits
better with a spare diet than with fashion." Perhaps young
Brandeis had heard the adage from the traditional service
in which Uncle Dembitz was so expert—*Marbeh nechasim,
marbeh deagah,* "Increase possessions, increase worry."

*

Mr. Brandeis had made his decision—he was to be free.
But free to what end? Was he to retire to the solitude of
his own study and watch society drift to chaos? Was he
to escape to Tarshish and leave Nineveh to perish because of
its iniquities? "What shall it profit a man if he save himself and see the whole world go lost?" Noah in Heaven, so
the Midrash weaves a fancy tale, regales the righteous with
accounts of his exploits in the building of the Ark and how
he escaped from the deluge that overwhelmed his con-
temporaries. "Little merit, old Noah," Moses frowns. "You
saved yourself—how about your generation?"

Mr. Brandeis changed the nature of his practice, restricted his manner of living, only to help his fellow-men.

*

The American adventure was not intended merely to provide fortunes for the few. It was meant to bring liberty and
happiness to the many. We were not exploiting the conti-
nent for the purpose of streaming it with rails and silhouet-
ting it with skyscrapers. The Founding Fathers wanted to
build men. What good is rapid material development if it

leads to the stultifying of mind and soul? What good is the
vote in the hands of hungry, ignorant, abject, timid crea-
tures? What good is citizenship, if it means meager opportunity for the child and no security for the old?

When Mr. Brandeis went out to his brethren toward the
end of the last century, he saw conditions that appalled
and saddened him. He could not reconcile the intent of
the Constitution and the Declaration of Independence, and
the purpose of the heroic struggle of the country's pioneers,
with what his eyes beheld. On the one side, unlimited
wealth; on the other, economic slavery that was crushing
the very desire for freedom. What was the advantage of
American democracy?

*

Mr. Brandeis soon realized that political liberty was not
enough. The Fathers had only won a major conflict; they
had not won the war. That was left to posterity. "We must
fight," Mr. Brandeis wrote, "for economic and industrial
freedom even as they had fought for political freedom,
for in a machine age, in a complex industrial society it is
far more indispensable even than political liberty." And
as the "people's attorney," Mr. Brandeis continued the war
of the Fathers. Our younger generation, that hears only of
the recluse Supreme Court Justice, so proverbially *wort-
karg,* cannot possibly visualize the Brandeis of forty or
forty-five years ago, the flaming spirit, the undaunted re-
former, employing the language of the prophet instead of
that of the jurist. Mr. Justice Holmes remembered him as
having that "crusading spirit, declaiming like one of those
upward and onward fellows." Mr. Brandeis was merciless
in his attack on the control exercised by investment bankers
over railroads, public service industry, banks, life insurance,
and trust companies. He pointed to the increasing number
of interlocking directorates as the root of many evils. "It
offends," he said, "laws human and divine."

Mr. Brandeis stood no more in awe of wealth than did Amos of Tekoa, and spoke with as little restraint as did Micah of Moreshet. There was prophetic tradition back of him and the fire of prophecy inside him. In his preface to the first volume of his *History of the Jewish People*, Renan writes: "In the realm of the intellectual and moral, Greece showed one deficiency but it was considerable. Greece despised the humble and felt no need for a god of justice. Its philosophers were dreaming of the immortality of the soul but were tolerant of the evils of this world. . . . The fervent genius of a small tribe established in a remote corner of Syria seemed to have come into the world to make up for this defect in the Hellenic character. Israel could never be satisfied to see the world badly governed under the government of Him whom they knew to be just. Its sages experienced a paroxysm of wrath in the presence of the abuses in which the world abounds. 'A wicked man dying old, rich and in peace, sent a twitch of pain and anger to their hearts.'" Poverty in the midst of plenty, economic slavery in a land with a democratic heritage, sent a twinge of pain and anger to the heart of Louis D. Brandeis. He was saddened when he reflected that the progress of science, the growth of invention, the development of industry, were not making for more happiness or freedom. "We are generating new forces without regard to corresponding controls. These forces are crushing the very spirit of freedom. There is frightful human waste. American democracy is being betrayed." Something was happening that was converting all the blessings of science and industry into a curse.

*

Mr. Brandeis drank deep from the fountain of liberty. He studied and mused long over the ideals of those who fashioned the republic. "How can we preserve our institutions and our ideals?" he asked, and even as Hillel or Rabbi Akiba, he answered, "Through the law." So he searched the law of the land and found that the freedom and opportunity of the individual were its highest promise. He was further instructed that the best laws were not "those by which men become more prosperous, but those by which they become most virtuous in character and best fitted for citizenship." Mr. Brandeis concluded that the great achievement of the English-speaking people is the attainment of liberty through the law. Abundant life, a Pharisee had said, was the purpose of the law. And a younger colleague added—"The law aims to refine man."

*

Systems and laws can change far more rapidly than human beings. Means of transportation can be outmoded more rapidly than habits of life. It takes more wisdom to build a new heart than to invent a new radio. Science has made progress in the things man uses. Science, religion, philosophy, and art have effected little change in the things by which men live. Progress depends on knowledge, wisdom, discipline, on laws, not only the laws man makes but the laws men obey. "Progress," Justice Brandeis said, "was slow. It required groping, experimentation. Therefore, knowledge was necessary, and therefore nothing happened that could wholly shake [my] faith."

*

Anti-Semitism obscured the grandeur of Zionism and, as is the case with all ideals, its essence was tarnished by the exigencies of fulfillment. Assimilationists and visionaries saw Zionism either as a movement of escape or as an extra encumbrance on the road to universalism. Idealists despised it because of its political entanglements. Justice Brandeis came to it because all his life he had been an uncompromising realist. He saw the world as it is, which means that he

examined, in any given situation, all of the facts insofar as
it was humanly possible to do so. The jumping board for
his intellectual efforts was not a formula or postulate but a
set of facts. He never theorized and rarely gave utterance
to an abstract principle or cosmic generalization. It was not
due, as some would want us to believe, to an absence of
faith or deficiency of style. Justice Brandeis' life's work is
incomprehensible without an absorbing faith in definite
principles and his "gift of happy phrasing was not incom-
parable to Holmes'." If Brandeis did not indulge in grandi-
ose, philosophic statements about the universe, it was because, in his opinion, every such statement would have
had to be based on all of the facts about the universe.
Experience had taught him that it required endless toil and
time to gather the data relative to the simplest human problem, let alone the cosmic. His Zionism consequently did
not derive from theory but from the Jewish people.

What were the facts respecting Zionism which this
realist could not possibly dismiss once they had come to
his attention? The first discovery Brandeis made was the
Jewish people. "It is of the nature of our law," he had said,
"that it has not dealt with man in general, but with him in
relationships." A Jew, too, he came to understand, had to
be dealt with in such terms. These relationships were not
only economic or political in character, but also social,
psychic, hereditary. It was not likely that in the real world
any man could be found suspended in isolation, after the
manner of Melchizedek, without father or mother, without
beginning or end. The individual, to be properly understood
in all of his relations, had to be seen also as the confluent
sum of the consciousness of, or, in the words of Dewey, as
nature's experiment with the qualities of the group. Brandeis
was persuaded by the "logic of realities" that what was true
of all human beings was most probably applicable to Jews.
Jews, too, he decided, belonged to a group or people.

Now, it is the nature of a fact to be so obvious and simple that only the genius can observe it, grasp it and hold on to it in its obviousness and simplicity. Mediocre minds tend either to distort it or overlay it with fiction or lose it altogether. What, for example, is more obvious than the existence of millions of men, women and children over the face of the earth to whom the myriad of millions of their fellowmen refer as Jews. The reference is ever immediate and direct and not the result of effort or inquiry. It is not discarded even when the discovery is made that the person designated as a Jew is without any religious faith or is a member of a Christian Church. Normally, that would seem to constitute ample proof of the existence of a Jewish folk or people. And yet it is amazing how many practical men, bankers, industrialists, merchants, and not a few philosophers and rabbis managed to miss the point. It required, among American Jews, a Brandeis to recognize it.

It was the recognition of this simple but ineluctable fact that led Justice Brandeis to Zionism. Genius that he was, he appreciated that it was no mean discovery. When later he read Herzl, he concluded that the major contribution of the father of political Zionism to the understanding of the Jewish problem was "the recognition of the fundamental fact that the Jews are a people, one people." Still later, he learned that the Jews had known it through their long history but that "it had been submerged by the multiform individual struggle for Jewish existence."

It was fortunate for Zionism that Brandeis had discovered simultaneously the Jewish people and both its precious heritage and unparalleled experience. For it was the Jewish laborer who brought him to Zionism, and it was Labor that in a large measure gave his Zionism that glow and passion of the last several years of his life. When in 1914 he accepted the chairmanship of the Zionist Provisional Emergency Committee he said, with the humility so characteristic of his whole life, "I feel my disqualification for this task. Throughout long years, which represent my own life, I have been to a great extent separated from Jews. I am very ignorant in things Jewish." What gave him the courage to assume the responsibility was that he found among Jewish laborers qualities of justice and democracy, a deep moral feeling, a deep sense of the brotherhood of man, and high intelligence.

At one of the many heated sessions of the Committee on Arbitration of the International Ladies' Garment Workers, a pale-looking laborer with high forehead and eyes full of indignation hurled a mouthful of strange words at one of the employers. The meaning of the words escaped Brandeis, but not the crimson flush that covered the employer to his ear lobes. When the meeting was adjourned, Brandeis, upon inquiry, learned that the magic words which had had such instantaneous effect were a quotation from the Book of Isaiah. The pale-faced young man had quoted: "What mean ye that ye beat my people to pieces, and grind the faces of the poor . . . The spoil of the poor is in your houses." Brandeis was stunned. A disbelieving laborer from whose lips the Hebrew of Isaiah rolled off with such ease and earnestness, a stubborn employer whose heart was pierced quickly and painfully by these words, was a novel experience indeed. He could not drive it from his mind. There was more to it, he felt certain, than appeared on the surface. The impression the young man had made, he decided, was not due to a display of erudition. Neither could the reference to Isaiah have been an isolated incident. It seemed to him to indicate a habit of life and a common background for the employer and employee.

Brandeis was soon convinced that he had guessed right. At subsequent meetings, in the midst of a heated harangue, he would hear a man shout with singular emphasis, *"Ihr darft sich shemen! Passt sich dos far a idin?"* (Shame on you! Is this conduct worthy of a Jew?) Brandeis was disturbed. About that time, December 10, 1910, the Jews of Boston were surprised to see the name of Louis Dembitz Brandeis appended to the following statement:

> "I have a great deal of sympathy for the [Zionist] movement, and I am deeply interested in the outcome of the propaganda. These so-called dreamers are entitled to the respect and appreciation of the entire Jewish people. . . . I believe the Jews can be just as much of a priest people today as they ever were in the prophetic days."

It was his first observation on the Jewish people. It was intuitive, a leap in the dark, the pull of heredity. The cautious Brandeis had not yet examined the facts, but it was inevitable that he should. Isaiah at an arbitration table! What was this unique background that had its hold both on employer and employee? The matter merited and importuned investigation.

He began to study his people. He returned to the Bible with renewed interest, and saw it in a new light. It was no longer for him a catechism of outmoded dogmas but the record of a people's striving to know and be itself. A Christian friend recalled that when Mr. Brandeis first appeared on the Zionist platform his face "shone with an inner light that transformed his whole being." It may be added that he was similarly transformed when he discovered the affinity between his own views and the prophetic-Pharisaic amalgam.

Need any reader of Brandeis be told how that pragmatic idealist reacted, say, to the following teachings or commonplaces of Judaism: Education must continue throughout life. Neither advanced age nor illness relieved a man of his obligation to learn. Study superseded everything. The whole system of Halachah is in essence factual and not conceptual.

Judges must be sticklers for facts as were Rabbi Johanan ben
Zakkai and his successors. To qualify as a member of the
Sanhedrin it was not sufficient that the candidate be expert
in the law but master of all knowledge attainable as well.
Utopia was not a spatial but a temporal concept. It was not
another Arcadia to which one might buy passage, but an
"end of days" to be achieved only by the sweat and toil of
the human race. In the scale of values works stood higher
than faith, and discipline than preachment. A poor man
must not be favored in a trial. Society was best founded on
objective and definitive justice rather than on subjective
and whimsical mercy. The individual was not more important than society nor society than the individual, it being
imperative to balance the freedom of the one against his
duties to the other and vice versa. Read not "the writing of
God was graven [*harut*] on the tables [of the Law]," but
that the writing of God on the tables signified freedom
[*herut*]. None is free but he who is occupied with the law.

No, the young man's quotation at the arbitration table
had not been an accident. It was part of a heritage that
embodied the life experience, dreaming, and thinking of
the people. There was such a people, a Jewish people. They
lied who tried to deny its existence. The "people's advocate"
became also the Jewish people's advocate.

*

Mr. Brandeis will not be remembered because of the
originality of his philosophy. He leaves behind no ponder-
ous, iron-clad system of irrefutable and imperishable
theories. The man was too modest and too practical for
such conceits. Then again his faith had never failed him
and his world had never become a "waste land" strewn with
broken images and withered stumps of time. He gladly
accepted the eternal verities. The Prophets, Tom Paine,
Thomas Jefferson, the Declaration of Independence, the

Constitution, and Abraham Lincoln sufficed him. He was not in search of the nebulous trail of ultimates. He did not believe that our society was diseased because of a want of philosophy. Neither would he concede that our spiritual disorganization and communal dislocation could be remedied by some new-fangled ideology or ex-machina creed. He was of the opinion that the Jewish, Christian, American heritage contained the wherewithal with which in due time to heal and reconstruct society. Mr. Brandeis will be remembered because he insisted that fine execution was no less important than speculation and the techniques of implementation were no less essential than faith itself. His never-failing optimism derived from this assumption, and from his own ability to devise social controls for social amelioration.

Mr. Brandeis was the typical and rarest representative of his time. He was of the world, modern, and of the scientific temper, but he also remained distant and aloof, and never became the slave of mechanical devices. Indeed, Mr. Brandeis was never the slave of anything or anyone. No passion, habit, hobby, or caprice could claim him. He was the master of all that assailed or beckoned or surged through him. In the realm of his being he was as absolute as the ruler of a totalitarian state. The French poet, Vigny, wrote that Destiny directs one half of a man's life, and that his character does the other half. Of Mr. Brandeis, one is tempted to say that his character was the arbiter of his destiny. And this perhaps was the secret and essence of the man.

Mr. Brandeis was as noble a Pharisee as ever lived. He adhered to a *Shulhan Aruch* as piously and unfalteringly as did Rabbi Akiba, Rabbi Joseph Karo, or Rabbi Moses Isserles. "Jews," he once asserted almost in the very language of these men and with the earnestness that characterized them, "who know the ritual law should understand that there can be no compromise between clean and unclean things." In his later years he frequently spoke with reverence of "our Torah." Shiftless men, the playthings of desire and devotees of the ephemeral, gaped in wonderment at his unswerving fidelity to his code of conduct. Superficial modernists, men of easy conscience, dilettanti, and cynics mocked his attention to detail, his stubborn insistence on efficiency, and his adamant resistance to compromise. But this was the man. No appraisal of his career, or evaluation of his character, or appreciation of his personality are conceivable or possible without due consideration of this Pharisaic, puritanic, Gibraltar-like quality of his.

Mr. Brandeis was a modern of the moderns. He followed with absorbing interest the development of science, expansion of industry, and increase of civilization. But he was apprehensive of what men generally describe as progress. He had read in the Psalms: "Except the LORD build the house they labor in vain that build it." He had heard Emerson say that "No institution will be better than the institutor." And he concluded that science was a fraud, industry a curse, and civilization a misnomer, if they did not serve to make men free. For Mr. Brandeis was not a pagan. Intellectual enjoyment and aesthetic delight when divorced from goodness were not for him the *summum bonum*.

In this regard too Mr. Brandeis was Hebraic, in the prophetic tradition. The existence of slums darkened for him the brilliance of universities and the splendor of museums. The skill of the machine and the magnitude of production were no atonement for the exploitation of labor. Philosophy, art, science, industry, government were not to develop, as it were, in a vacuum unrelated to one another and unconcerned with society. They were to function for the welfare of man. Progress was not that which was contemporary or new or ingenious or the latest mechanical device. Progress was that which was consistent with "human truths" and human freedom.

Mr. Brandeis' whole career is an object lesson in freedom. He lived as if he had all his days set out to prove freedom's meaning, purpose, and beauty. He learned early that freedom consisted not solely of the removal of external authority but in an intelligent exercise of the will. It was not the gift of the gods but the fruit of diligent and patient discipline. "There were more things which Diogenes would have refused, than there were which Alexander could have given or enjoyed." Men were free if they could maintain their conscience and adhere to their code against the pressure of immediate desires, if they could cultivate their highest faculties at the expense of the lower. As long as we are enmeshed in tangled thickets of sensual and conventional living we were not free. Mr. Brandeis desired freedom more than anything in life and he achieved it through the exercise of the will. He rose above the temptations that compass us on every side. He lived in Spartan simplicity from conviction. No force on earth could make him alter his way of life. The social whirl of Boston or Washington saddened him. It never attracted him. Not that he was unsocial, cool, ascetic, or even austere. Only those who did not know him or those who could not resist the pull of fashion thought of him in that light. Those who saw him at close range found him conversable, warm, simple, and gracious. A child felt as much at home with him as did the sage. His life was ordered and disciplined, not because he was by inclination or temperament a hermit or recluse. Quite the contrary is true. Mr. Brandeis desired to live abundantly. But he realized that life could not possibly be abundant unless it was free.

It was his love of freedom and even more his possession of it that made him the consecrated American he was. His patriotism reached down to the roots of his being. For America was not only bread, raiment, and hearth; it was "the world's best hope," the experiment par excellence in democracy, i.e., in freedom. Mr. Brandeis had taken long drafts from Roger Williams, Jefferson, Lincoln, Whitman. He understood what the first and later Fathers of the Republic had taken the core of Americanism to be. They had not come here, they had not fought England, they had not set brother against brother in order that we might become the richest and most powerful nation on the face of the earth. They toiled and bled that we might enjoy the blessings of liberty. Mr. Brandeis followed the thorny path. He risked all, the distinguished career he had achieved at an earlier age than most men, the friends he had made, the quiet he loved, and his very reputation to recapture for America's masses the freedom that unparalleled industrial expansion had deadened. For years he was a target of abuse, calumny, hatred. Men of power and prominence rose up against him to devour him. Of him, alas for the interested perverseness of man, five United States Senators wrote, "One whose reputation for honesty and integrity among his associates has proved to be bad, which reputation has been justified by his own conduct." Mr. Brandeis did not flinch; he suffered ecstatically as any martyr does for his faith. He was an American, and of Americans Washington testified that their love of liberty was interwoven with every ligament of their hearts.

It was this traditional conception of America and his deep attachment to freedom that brought him closer to the Jewish people. No sooner did he come face to face with Jews than he grasped the uniqueness of their history. Here was a strange phenomenon, a burning bush that was not consumed, a despised and tormented people that chose to live, to live and be itself. When the true cause of Israel's martyrdom flashed upon him, he became a resolute and confident Jew. For the history of Israel is eccentric and its martyrdom vain if it is not one long struggle for freedom. The Jew is not genuine if he is not the bravest soldier on the battlefield of liberty. His experience is unilateral, restricted, written into one covenant, that kings and rulers, mobs and majorities shall not lord it over the consciences of their brethren.

After turning the pages of the Bible, Graetz, and Herzl, Mr. Brandeis realized that his people's huge affliction was the result of continuous resistance to world trusts. Because Israel was small and weak it was not yet sufficient reason why it should be swallowed up by the many and mighty. Sheer bigness was a curse. God had called Amos from Tekoa and Lincoln from Gentryville. Mr. Brandeis recognized in the shepherd of Tekoa the spiritual father of the rail-splitter from Gentryville. Lincoln unsheathed the sword to preserve justice and freedom. Israel suffered martyrdom to maintain its cause and conscience.

It was a great day for Mr. Brandeis when he discovered that Americanism and Judaism were of one pattern.

PART TWO

THE WORDS OF
JUSTICE BRANDEIS

✳

ABNORMAL AND PRIVILEGED

In every society there must be some who are abnormal, and some who are blinded by privilege. One cannot properly feel even indignation at either. They are rather subjects for sympathy. But we must seek steadily to nullify their influence, and limit their numbers.

ABSOLUTE

Nobody ought to be absolute; everybody ought to be protected from arbitrariness and wrong decisions by the representations of others who are being affected.

ABSOLUTE POWER

The objections to despotism and monopoly are fundamental in human nature. They rest upon the innate and ineradicable selfishness of man. They rest upon the fact that absolute power inevitably leads to abuse.[1]

---

[1] See also Monopoly.

ABSTRACT THINKING

Abstractions are frequently attractive, ingenious, and valuable. But ever so often abstract thinking borders on mysticism. Whenever that happens I have a feeling that reason rests and imagination takes over.

A DAY'S WORK

[5] I rise early because no day is long enough for a day's work.

AGREEMENT

Every agreement curtails the liberty of those who enter into it.

AMENDING THE CONSTITUTION

I see no need to amend our Constitution. It has not lost its capacity for expansion to meet new conditions, unless it be interpreted by rigid minds which have no such capacity. Instead of amending the Constitution, I would amend men's economic and social ideals.

AMENDMENT

A code of law that makes no provision for its amendment provides for its ultimate rejection.

AMERICA

America, dedicated to liberty and the brotherhood of man, rejected the aristocratic principle of the superman as applied to peoples as it rejected the principle when applied to individuals. America has believed that each race had something of peculiar value which it can contribute to the attainment of those high ideals for which it is striving. America has believed that we must not only give to the immigrant the best that we have, but must preserve for America the good that is in the immigrant and develop in him the best of which he is capable. America has believed that in differentiation, not in uniformity, lies the path of progress.[2] It acted on this belief; it has advanced human happiness, and it has prospered.

*

[10] We have slipped back badly in twenty-five years, in order, security to life and property; in liberty of speech, action and assembly; in culture; and, in many respects, in morality. Father would have said: "Pfui."

*

We shall learn most by unprejudiced painstaking study of our own strengths and weaknesses; by enquiry into our own achievements and shortcomings. It is thus that we may best learn how great are the possibilities of high accomplishments in the future; what are the real dangers with which we shall be confronted.

*

America, which seeks "the greatest good of the greatest number," cannot be content with conditions that fit only the hero, the martyr or the slave.[3]

America in the last century proved that democracy is a success.[4]

AMERICAN DEMOCRACY

American democracy rests upon the basis of the free citizen.[5]

AMERICAN IDEALS [6]

[15] What are the American ideals? They are the development of the individual for his own and the common good;

---

[2] Repeated under Differentiation Not Uniformity.
[3] Repeated under Greatest Good of Greatest Number.
[4] Repeated under Industrial Democracy and Thinking.
[5] Repeated under Financial Dependence.
[6] See also Conservation.

the development of the individual through liberty, and the attainment of the common good through democracy and social justice.

Our form of government, as well as humanity, compels us to strive for the development of the individual man. Under universal suffrage (soon to be extended to women) every voter is a part ruler of the state. Unless the rulers have, in the main, education and character, and are free men, our great experiment in democracy must fail. It devolves upon the state, therefore, to fit its rulers for their task. It must provide not only facilities for development but the opportunity of using them. It must not only provide opportunity, it must stimulate the desire to avail of it. Thus we are compelled to insist upon the observance of what we somewhat vaguely term the American standard of living; we become necessarily our brothers' keepers.[7]

*

Manhood is what we are striving for in America. We are striving for democracy; we are striving for the development of men. It is absolutely essential in order that men may develop that they be properly fed and properly housed, and that they have proper opportunities of education and recreation. We cannot reach our goal without those things. But we may have all those things and have a nation of slaves.

*

We Americans are committed not only to social justice in the sense of avoiding things which bring suffering and harm, like unjust distribution of wealth; but we are committed primarily to democracy. The social justice for which we are striving is an incident of our democracy, not the main end. It is rather the result of democracy—perhaps its finest

---

[7] See also Brotherhood, Greatest Good of Greatest Number.

expression—but it rests upon democracy, which implies the rule by the people.[8]

*

Our American ideals cannot be attained unless an end is put to the misery due to poverty.[9]

AMERICANIZATION

What is Americanizaiton? It manifests itself, in a superficial way, when the immigrant adopts the clothes, the manners and the customs generally prevailing here. Far more important is the manifestation presented when he substitutes for his mother tongue the English language as the common medium of speech. But the adoption of our language, manners and customs is only a small part of the process. To become Americanized the change wrought must be fundamental. However great his outward conformity, the immigrant is not Americanized unless his interests and affections have become deeply rooted here. And we properly demand of the immigrant even more than this—he must be brought into complete harmony with our ideals and aspirations and cooperate with us for their attainment. Only when this has been done will he possess the national consciousness of an American.

AMERICAN JEWISH COMMUNITY[10]

[20]   I have not given much thought to the future of the American Jewish community. Perhaps because I was sure that it will always be there. Assimilation will undoubtedly make inroads. But what of it? Have not persecution, conversion, and indifference claimed their victims? The character and fortitude of those who will survive will more than

---

[8] Repeated under Industrial Democracy.
[9] Repeated under Efficiency and Social Ideals.
[10] See also Noblesse Oblige.

make up for the losses the American Jewish community will suffer.

AMERICANS

There is in most Americans some spark of idealism, which can be fanned into a flame. It takes sometimes a divining rod to find what it is; but when found, and that means often, when disclosed to the owners, the results are often most extraordinary.

AMERICAN STANDARD OF LIVING

What does this standard imply: In substance, the exercise of those rights which our Constitution guarantees—the right to life, liberty and the pursuit of happiness. Life, in this connection, means living, not existing; liberty, freedom in things industrial as well as political; happiness includes, among other things, that satisfaction which can come only through the full development and utilization of one's faculties.

AMERICA'S FUNDAMENTAL LAW

America's fundamental law seeks to make real the brotherhood of man.[11]

AMERICA'S INSISTENT DEMAND

America's insistent demand in the twentieth century is for social justice.[11]

ANGELS AND DEVILS

[25] Those who have given up the belief in witchcraft must be hard put to explain their continued belief in the existence of angels and devils.

ANTI-SEMITISM AND THE NAZIS

Prior to the advent of Nazism we used to think that anti-Semitism was the Jewish people's misfortune and the world's

---

[11] Repeated under Jewish Spirit and America.

disgrace. The Nazis have convinced many that anti-Semitism can also be a boomerang.

ARBITRATION

I believe that arbitration is going to be a comparatively insignificant factor in the prevention and settlement of trade disputes. Arbitration implies and involves the shirking of responsibility by the chief parties to the dispute. The burden of the task of adjustment is shifted onto the shoulders of some alien tribunal. The result is that employer and workman fail to get the discipline they ought to have, and they are prevented from obtaining that intimate insight into one another's needs and difficulties without which essential justice is likely to be missed.

But beyond that, the arbitrators are rather likely, from the very nature of their task, to hand down a wrong award. They may easily miss the heart of the difficulty, because they are not in the midst of the actual struggle. No, I do not anticipate any very great results, in the long run, from arbitration. . . .

The best of all is . . . strong unions and direct adjustment between employer and workmen.

ARGUMENT OF FORCE

Silence coerced by law—the argument of force in its worst form.[12]

ARITHMETIC

Mellen was a masterful man, resourceful, courageous, broad of view. He fired the imagination of New England, but being oblique of vision merely distorted its judgment and silenced its conscience. For a while he triumphed with impunity over laws human and divine, but as he was obsessed with the delusion that two and two make five he fell

---

[12] Repeated under Freedom of Speech.

at last a victim of the relentless rules of humble arithmetic.

Remember, O Stranger!

Arithmetic is the first of the sciences and the mother of safety.

*

[30]   Figures—a language implying certitude.

ART

Living among things of beauty is a help toward culture and the life worth-while.

ARTIFICIAL LEGAL CONVICTION

No instance has been found where under our law a fact-finding body has been required to give to evidence an effect which it does not inherently possess. Proof implies persuasion. To compel the human mind to infer in any respect that which observation and logic tells us is not true interferes with the process of reasoning of the fact-finding body. It would be a departure from the unbroken practice to require an artificial legal conviction where no real conviction exists.

ARTISTS

Though the work of the greatest artists may command the highest prices, their incentive has not been money. It has been the desire to achieve professional success.[13]

AVERAGES

I abhor averages. I like the individual case. A man may have six meals one day and none the next, making an average of three per day, but that is not a good way to live.

BANKER-MIDDLEMAN[14]

[35]   The investment banker has, within his legitimate province, acquired control so extensive as to menace the public

---

[13] Repeated under Money-making and Service.
[14] See also People's Own Gold.

welfare, even where his business is properly conducted. If the New Freedom is to be attained, every proper means of lessening that power must be availed of. A simple and effective remedy, which can be widely applied, even without new legislation, lies near at hand:—Eliminate the banker-middleman where he is superfluous.

BANKERS' ETHICS

The organization of the Money Trust is intensive, the combination comprehensive; but no other element was recognized as necessary to render it stable, and to make its dynamic force irresistible. Despotism, be it financial or political, is vulnerable, unless it is believed to rest upon a moral sanction.[15] The longing for freedom is ineradicable. It will express itself in protest against servitude and inaction, unless the striving for freedom be made to seem immoral. Long ago monarchs invented, as a preservative of absolutism, the fiction of "The divine right of kings." Bankers, imitating royalty, invented recently that precious rule of so-called "Ethics," by which it is declared unprofessional to come to the financial relief of any corporation which is already the prey of another "reputable" banker. . . .

The "Ethical" basis of the rule must be that the interests of the combined bankers are superior to the interests of the rest of the community. Their attitude reminds one of the "spheres of influence" with ample "hinterlands" by which rapacious nations are adjusting differences.[16]

BANKERS' FAILURE

This failure of banker-management is not surprising. The surprise is that men should have supposed it would succeed. For banker-management contravenes the fundamental laws of human limitations: *First*, that no man can serve two mas-

---

[15] Repeated under Despotism.
[16] See also Monopoly.

ters; *second*, that a man cannot at the same time do many things well.

BANKERS' FUNCTION

It is not the proper function of the banker to construct, purchase, or operate railroads, or to engage in industrial enterprises. The proper function of the banker is to give to or to withhold credit from other concerns; to purchase or to refuse to purchase securities from other concerns; and to sell securities to other customers. The proper exercise of this function demands that the banker should be wholly detached from the concern whose credit or securities are under consideration. His decision to grant or to withhold credit, to purchase or not to purchase securities, involves passing judgment on the efficiency of the management or the soundness of the enterprise; and he ought not to occupy a position where in so doing he is passing judgment on himself. Of course detachment does not imply lack of knowledge. The banker should act only with full knowledge, just as a lawyer should act only with full knowledge. The banker who undertakes to make loans to or purchase securities from a railroad for sale to his other customers ought to have as full knowledge of its affairs as does its legal adviser. But the banker should not be, in any sense, his own client. He should not, in the capacity of banker, pass judgment upon the wisdom of his own plans or acts as railroad man.

Such a detached attitude on the part of the banker is demanded also in the interest of his other customers—the purchasers of corporate securities. The investment banker stands toward a large part of his customers in a position of trust, which should be fully recognized. The small investors, particularly the women, who are holding an ever-increasing proportion of our corporate securities, commonly buy on the recommendation of their bankers. The small investors do not, and in most cases cannot, ascertain for themselves the facts on which to base a proper judgment as to the soundness of securities offered. And even if these investors were furnished with the facts, they lack the business experience essential to forming a proper judgment. Such investors need and are entitled to have the bankers' advice, and obviously their unbiased advice; and the advice cannot be unbiased where the banker, as part of the corporation's management, has participated in the creation of the securities which are the subject of sale to the investor.

BANKERS' POWER[17]

The bankers' power grows by what it feeds on. Power begets wealth; and added wealth opens ever new opportunities for the acquisition of wealth and power. The operations of these bankers are so vast and numerous that even a very reasonable compensation for the service performed by the bankers would, in the aggregate, produce for them incomes so large as to result in huge accumulations of capital. But the compensation taken by the bankers as commissions or profits is often far from reasonable. Occupying, as they so frequently do, the inconsistent position of being at the same time seller and buyer, the standard for so-called compensation actually applied is not the "Rule of reason," but "All the traffic will bear." And this is true even where there is no sinister motive. The weakness of human nature prevents men from being good judges of their own deservings.[18]

BETRAYAL OF OUR GREAT HERITAGE

[40]   We cannot afford to be represented by men who are dishonest and reckless to the great heritage of an honorable, glorious past, handed down to us by our fathers.

---

[17] See also Interlocking Directorates.
[18] Repeated under Human Nature.

BETTER THAN PEACE

There is something better than peace, and that is the peace that is won by struggle.[19]

BIBLE

The Bible first attracted me because of its plainness of speech, its insistence on the righteousness of the individual and justice of the group, the unrestraint with which it arraigns the Jewish people and its patriarchs and chosen leaders. I wonder whether any government today would risk publishing a document depicting the nation's most favored ruler as the Bible does David. I doubt whether there is anything in the authorized and approved annals of the nations comparable to the rapid review of the lives of the kings found in the Book of Kings, particularly to that terrifying brief verse, "And he did that which was evil in the sight of the LORD: he departed not all his days from the sins of Jeroboam the son of Nebat, wherewith he made Israel to sin."

The Bible is great as wisdom and law, and greatest as prophecy. Greatest because rarest. Man somehow gropes his way to wisdom and law. But he no sooner acquires them, than he abuses them. He does not live by them of his own free will. He must be driven to do so. He must be accused and lashed when he ignores them. But this can be done only by those who are themselves above reproach and prepared to face martyrdom. Such men are rare. And such men were the Prophets. They denounced the follies and crimes of their own kings and people as they did of the mightiest empires of their day. They ridiculed the boastfulness of dictators as daringly as they did the inertness of idols. Add to this their abiding faith in man's goodness, their optimism and visions of a world living in peace, security, and brother-

---

[19] Repeated under Vital and Beyond Price.

hood, the unmatched power and beauty of their language, and they stand alone among the benefactors of the human race. It is no exaggeration to say that they are still the first to reprove us when we go astray. I think that many people employ the expression "an Old Testament prophet" as a synonym for conscience.[20]

BIG BUSINESS [21]

"Big business" will then mean business big not in bulk or power, but great in service and grand in manner.

BIGNESS [22]

There used to be a certain glamour about big things. Anything big, simply because it was big, seemed to be good and great. We are now coming to see that big things may be very bad and mean.

*

[45]   Size, we are told, is not a crime. But size may, at least, become noxious by reason of the means through which it was attained or the uses to which it is put.

*

The evils of bigness are something different from and additional to the evils of monopoly. A business may be too big to be efficient without being a monopoly; and it may be a monopoly and yet (so far as size is concerned) may be well within the limits of efficiency.

*

When . . . you increase your business to a very great extent, and the multitude of problems increase with its

---

[20] The hour struck 9 A.M. The conversation ended abruptly. When I next came to the Brandeis home, October 7, 1941, in the company of Judge Louis E. Levinthal, it was to attend his funeral service.
[21] See also Industrial Liberty, Monopoly.
[22] See also Monopoly.

growth, you will find, in the first place, that the man at the head has a diminishing knowledge of the facts and, in the second place, a diminishing opportunity of exercising a careful judgment upon them. Furthermore—and this is one of the most important grounds of inefficiency of large institutions—there develops a centrifugal force greater than the centripetal force. Demoralization sets in; a condition of lessened efficiency presents itself. . . . These are disadvantages that attend bigness.

*

In all human institutions there must be a limit of greatest efficiency. . . . Everybody in his experience knows his own limitations; knows how much less well he can do many things than a few things. There undoubtedly is a limit with a railroad, as in the case of other institutions, where they may be too small; but there is another limit where they may be too large—where the centrifugal force will be greater than the centripetal, and where, by reason of the multiplicity of problems and the distance to the circumference, looseness of administration arises that overcomes any advantage from size, overcomes it so far as to make it relatively a losing proposition.[23]

*

The successful, the powerful trusts, have created conditions absolutely inconsistent with these—America's—industrial and social needs. It may be true that as a legal proposition mere size is not a crime, but mere size may become an industrial and social menace, because it frequently creates as against possible competitors and as against the employees conditions of such gross inequality, as to imperil the welfare of the employees and of the industry.

---

[23] See also Organization.

BLIGHTING INFLUENCE OF
JOURNALISTIC GOSSIP[24]

[50]   The press is overstepping in every direction the obvious bounds of propriety and of decency. Gossip is no longer
the resource of the idle and of the vicious, but has become a
trade, which is pursued with industry as well as effrontery.
To satisfy a prurient taste the details of sexual relations are
spread broadcast in the columns of the daily papers. To
occupy the indolent, column upon column is filled with idle
gossip, which can only be procured by intrusion upon the
domestic circle. The intensity and complexity of life, attendant upon advancing civilization, have rendered necessary
some retreat from the world, and man, under the refining
influence of culture, has become more sensitive to publicity,
so that solitude and privacy have become more essential to
the individual; but modern enterprise and invention have,
through invasions upon his privacy, subjected him to mental
pain and distress, far greater than could be inflicted by mere
bodily injury. Nor is the harm wrought by such invasions
confined to the suffering of those who may be made the subjects of journalistic or other enterprise. Each crop of un-
seemly gossip, thus harvested, becomes the seed of more,
and in direct proportion to its circulation, results in a lower-
ing of social standards and of morality. Even gossip apparently harmless, when widely and persistently circulated, is
potent for evil. It both belittles and perverts. It belittles by
inverting the relative importance of things, thus dwarfing
the thoughts and aspirations of a people. When personal
gossip attains the dignity of print, and crowds the space
available for matters of real interest to the community, what
wonder that the ignorant and thoughtless mistake its relative importance. Easy of comprehension, appealing to that
weak side of human nature which is never wholly cast down

---

[24] See also Propriety, Right to Privacy.

by the misfortunes and frailties of our neighbors,[25] no one can be surprised that it usurps the place of interest in brains capable of other things. Triviality destroys at once robustness of thought and delicacy of feeling. No enthusiasm can flourish, no generous impulse can survive under its blighting influence.[26]

BOLDNESS

Sometimes, if we would guide by the light of reason, we must let our minds be bold.[27]

BRAIN

The brain is like the hand. It grows with using.[28]

BROTHERHOOD [29]

There is one feature in our ideals and practices which is peculiarly American—it is inclusive brotherhood.

Other countries, while developing the individual man, have assumed that their common good would be attained only if the privileges of their citizenship should be limited practically to natives or to persons of a particular nationality. America, on the other hand, has always declared herself for equality of nationalities as well as for equality of individuals. It recognizes racial equality as an essential of full human liberty and true brotherhood, and that racial equality is the complement of democracy. America has, therefore, given like welcome to all the peoples of Europe.

*

The spirit which subordinates the interests of the individual to that of the class is the spirit of brotherhood—a near

---

[25] Repeated under Human Nature.
[26] Repeated under Triviality.
[27] Repeated under Experimentation.
[28] Repeated under Industrial Democracy and Thinking.
[29] See also American Ideals.

approach to altruism; it reaches pure altruism when it involves a sacrifice of present interests for the welfare of others
in the distant future.

BUSINESS—A PROFESSION [30]

[55]   Business should be, and to some extent already is, one
of the professions.

*

Why should not we recognize in the great realm of business those principles which have been the common property
of the most advanced thought? Every man in the medical
world glories in having given to the world something which
advances medical science. Every man in the field of architecture glories when he can give to the world something that
advances architectural science. You will find exactly the
same thing in almost every department of engineering. Why
should it not be so in business? Is there any lack of opportunity for competition, honorable competition, in the field
of engineering or of architecture or of medicine? They can
play the game wherever a man can see it. There need be no
secrets when it comes to the question of advancing the art
to which man devotes himself. And the same is absolutely
true of business and will be recognized as true of business as
soon as men come to recognize that business is one of the
noblest and most promising of all the professions.

BUSINESS SUCCESS

In the field of modern business, so rich in opportunity for
the exercise of man's finest and most varied mental faculties
and moral qualities, mere money-making cannot be regarded
as the legitimate end. Neither can mere growth in bulk or
power be admitted as a worthy ambition. Nor can a man
nobly mindful of his serious responsibilities to society, view

---

[30] See also Money-making and Service.

business as a game; since with the conduct of business human happiness or misery is inextricably interwoven.

Real success in business is to be found in achievements comparable rather with those of the artist or the scientist, of the inventor or the statesman. And the joys sought in the profession of business must be like their joys and not the mere vulgar satisfaction which is experienced in the acquisition of money, in the exercise of power or in the frivolous pleasure of mere winning.

CALMNESS

To the exercise of good judgment calmness is, in times of deep feeling and on subjects which excite passion, as essential as fearlessness and honesty.[31]

CAPACITY OF INDIVIDUAL MAN

Man's works have in many instances outrun the capacity of the individual man. For no matter how good the organization, the capacity of an individual man must ordinarily determine the success of a particular enterprise, not only financially to the owners, but in service to the community. Organization can do much to make possible larger efficient units; but organization can never be a substitute for initiative and for judgment.[32] These must be supplied by the chief executive officers, and nature sets a limit to their possible accomplishment.

CENTRALIZATION

[60] History teaches, I believe, that the present tendency toward centralization must be arrested, if we are to attain the American ideals, and that for it must be substituted intense development of life through activities in the several States and localities. The problem is a very difficult one, but

---

31 Repeated under Freedom of Speech.
32 Repeated under Organization.

the local University is the most hopeful instrument for any attempt at solution.

CHALLENGE OF EXISTING LAW

The challenge of existing law is not a manifestation peculiar to our country or to our time. Sporadic dissatisfaction has doubtless existed in every country at all times. Such dissatisfaction has usually been treated by those who govern as evidencing the unreasonableness of law breakers. The line "No thief e'er felt the halter draw with good opinion of the law," expresses the traditional attitude of those who are apt to regard existing law as "the true embodiment of everything that's excellent." It required the joint forces of Sir Samuel Romilly and Jeremy Bentham to make clear to a humane, enlightened and liberty-loving England that death was not the natural and proper punishment for theft. Still another century had to elapse before social science raised the doubt whether theft was not perhaps as much the fault of the community as of the individual.

In periods of rapid transformation, challenge of existing law, instead of being sporadic, becomes general. Such was the case in Athens . . . Germany . . . the recent dissatisfaction with our law as administered [has] been due, in large measure, to the fact that it had not kept pace with the rapid development of our political, economic and social ideals. In other words, . . . the challenge of legal justice [is] due to its failure to conform to contemporary conceptions of social justice.

CHANGE IN A DEMOCRACY

In a democratic community men who are to be affected by a proposed change of conditions should be consulted and the innovators must carry the burden of convincing others at each state of the process of change that what is being done is right.

CHARACTER

It is only in the Latin sense that talents are to be "admired"; they are to be wondered at. But character only is to be "admired" as we use that word. It is the effort—the attempt—that tells. Man's work is, at best, so insignificant compared with that of the Creator—it is all so Lilliputian, one cannot bow before it.[33]

CHARACTER AND INTELLIGENCE

Democratic ideals can be attained only where those who govern exercise their power not by alleged divine right or inheritance, but by force of character and intelligence.[34]

CHILD

[65]   Since the child is the father of the man, we must bear constantly in mind that the American standard of living cannot be attained or preserved unless the child is not only well fed but well born; unless he lives under conditions wholesome morally as well as physically; unless he is given education adequate both in quantity and in character to fit him for life's work.

CHOSEN PEOPLE [35,a]

That the Jews have regarded themselves as the chosen people is understandable. They were for a period of many centuries the only monotheists in the world.[b] They alone

---

[33] Repeated under Man's Work.
[34] Repeated under Democratic Ideals.
[35] See also Jews Today.
[a] I give here a summation of what the Justice said on the question of a "chosen people" on the several occasions I brought up the subject.
[b] When I mentioned the opinion of certain scholars to the effect that some primitive tribes were monotheists, the Justice countered that that was an abuse of language. For the monotheism of those tribes, he said, if it existed was unreasoned, as, for example, when a child speaks accidentally of war, or justice, or love. Furthermore, he argued, that brand of monotheism had obviously had little

had the idea of one invisible God who could not be represented in images.[c] They alone spoke with ever more insistence of a perpetual covenant with God. This, by the way,
seems to me to be the basic teaching of the Bible. God is
one and Israel is one and the two are bound together for
ever.[d]

True, all or most ancient peoples believed themselves to
be the favorites of certain gods. But I wonder whether the
relation was as firm and persistent. Anyway, the gods of the
Near East and the Graeco-Roman world collapsed and the
peoples disintegrated. Since the Jews and their God alone
escaped from the wreckage, it was natural that they should
grow closer to each other.

When the Western world was converted to Christianity
the belief in the election of Israel gathered new momentum.
For then everybody believed that Israel was a chosen people. If there was any difference of opinion it was only as to
the identity of Israel. We can hardly blame the Jews for
having resolved the matter in their favor. They knew themselves to be Israel and knew that everybody recognized
Israel as having been chosen by God.

Christian excesses against the Jews strengthened this conviction even more than did the collapse of the pagan gods
and pagan states. For the hounded and persecuted, finding
themselves more and more isolated, grew closer and closer
to their God and drew their God closer to themselves. Cer-

---

effect on those who professed it. When I suggested that some of the
Greek philosophers appeared to have been monotheists, he said that
that was most likely true, but that all the same the Greek people
remained polytheists.
[c] I mentioned the fact that the earliest Roman cult was imageless.
The Justice's comment was that the Jews had probably never heard
of it.
[d] I remarked that the *Zohar* spoke of God and Israel as being called
one when together, but not when parted. The Justice smiled with
satisfaction as he did whenever I interjected that there was support
in Jewish literature for what he was saying.

tainly the more vigorously the Church argued that it was
Israel and that it was God's elect, the faster the Jews held
on to their ancient belief.

So much I find reasonable and so much I understand.
Whether this in the last analysis is traceable to tribal self-
glorification, or whether it has done the Jews and the world
good or harm, is a question that requires the careful investigation of twenty-five centuries of history.

What, however, need not wait for the results of research
is the revision or reinterpretation, as you call it, of this belief.[e] That is, assuming that we wish to continue speaking
of ourselves as a chosen people.[f] When I ask for revision I
am not doing it because in recent years well-meaning liberals
discovered in the "dogma" of the election of Israel the roots
of Nazi race theories. That should give us no concern, except
insofar as we ought to open the eyes of the blind.

One of your colleagues [g] who was here several days ago
tried to reeducate me into anti-Zionism (He had mistakenly
assumed that because for many years my associations with
Jews were limited that I had been an anti-Zionist. As a
rabbi he should have known that most people are neither
for nor against. They're neutrals. And neutrality is at times
a graver sin than belligerence).[36, h] He began by saying that
Zionism made for anti-Semitism, and concluded that the

---

[e] I had often mentioned that Jewish scholars were engaged in re-
interpreting the past and that one of them, Professor Mordecai M.
Kaplan, had founded a movement on the basis of its reconstruction.
[f] I drew the Justice into this discussion by telling him that the concept of the chosen people had become a subject of controversy.
[g] The Justice did not mention the name of the rabbi and I did not
ask for it.
[36] Repeated under Neutrality.
[h] When I left the Brandeis home I thought that the Justice had
raised his voice when he spoke of neutrality. I believed that he had
in mind the neutrality of the United States, England, France, and
other world powers in the face of Nazi atrocities. He had spoken
feelingly of their inaction several days before.

Jews had always been mindful of what the Gentiles were saying.

I made no comment on his anti-Semitism argument. I said only that the Jews were mindful to maintain high standards of education, ethics, morality, etc., lest they defame the name of the God they claimed had chosen them.[i]

We cannot and should not be oblivious of world opinion but we certainly ought to be as attentive to what we have to say to the world as to what the world has to say to or of us. We must not permit the prejudiced and ignorant to shape our lives. The prejudiced will always call the best worst and the ignorant will confuse the two.

When I speak of revision it is because the idea of the chosen people cannot mean today what it was understood to mean in antiquity or the Middle Ages. There were too many barriers between peoples for them to get acquainted and see each other as they were. I doubt whether the ancient Babylonians had learned much from the Egyptians, or the Egyptians from them. That is, I doubt whether there was wide-spread knowledge of the arts of one among the other, or whether they read each other's literature or analyzed each other's beliefs and way of life.

I hesitate to express an opinion as to what our own people actually knew about the pagan peoples whom they condemned. My Bar Mitzvah,[j] I am told you once "informed against" me, was delayed to my 54th [k] year. But my impres-

---

[i] I quoted Ezekiel, XXXVI, 20: "And when they came unto the nations, whither they came, they profaned My holy name; in that men said of them: 'These are the people of the LORD, and are gone forth out of His land.'" The Justice reflected for a moment but made no comment.

[j] Hebrew for the "son of command" or "man of duty." Upon his thirteenth birthday a Jewish boy, according to Jewish tradition, reaches the age of duty and responsibility.

[k] At a mass celebration in honor of the Justice's seventy-fifth birthday I alluded to the fact that Mr. Brandeis had first discovered his people in 1910, when he was 54 years old, adding that that year

sion is that the Jews did not know much and perhaps took
lightly what they did know. Egypt was an enemy, and so
were Babylonia, Assyria, and the smaller neighboring states,
and all of them were idolaters.[1] Hellenism was shut out of
view by Antiochus Epiphanes and Roman civilization by
its procurators and by its two or three mad kings. And again
the Greeks and Romans were idolaters. I wonder whether an
intimate knowledge of the life and work of Socrates, Peri-
cles, Plato, and Aristotle might not have led the Rabbis to
modify their views of the pagan world, and with it their conception of a chosen people. According to Graetz there are
some kind words in Jewish sources for Alexander the Great
and some warm feelings for Julius Caesar. I do not recall to

---

should be remembered as the year of his Bar Mitzvah. I had the
privilege, on that occasion, of sharing the platform with Dr. Stephen
S. Wise and Justice Andrew A. Bruce, both of whom were close to
the Justice. I have had the feeling that one of them "informed
against" me. When we took tea after the meeting, Justice Bruce
evinced great interest in the institution of Bar Mitzvah.

[1] I pointed out that the Rabbis knew more about the Greeks and
Romans than was the general impression, that they used many Greek
and Latin loan-words, held the Greek language and culture in high
regard, were dazzled by the might and tumultuousness of the Roman
Empire, compared Rome to the sun, made it the goal of Moses and
David, and one of the Rabbis even praised the Romans for the roads,
aqueducts, and baths they had built everywhere. And some of them
may even have had some knowledge of Latin literature. I further
added that the Rabbis, however, saw through the duplicity of
Roman diplomacy and spoke bitterly of Roman barbaric acts and
the social inequality and injustice that prevailed in Rome itself.
R. Joshua b. Levi, I recalled, who had visited Rome, could not
forget the painful contrast between Roman treatment of marble
statues and the poor. The former, he noted, were covered with
expensive rugs to protect them against the winter's cold and the
summer's heat. The latter were left uncared for—to starve and
freeze. But, I concluded, it was probably undeniable that the
Rabbis' views of the Greeks were colored by the atrocities of Antiochus, and their views of Rome by the conviction that Rome was
the new Edom, the arch-enemy of Israel. The Justice remarked that
we probably get as distorted a view of Rome in rabbinic writings
as we do of the Pharisees in the New Testament.

what the historian attributes the fact. But I surmise that it was most probably due to the benevolence of which Alexander and Caesar were capable and their tolerance of beliefs and practices not their own.[m] In other words, a friendly idolater could be distinguished from a hostile one. Might it not be then that the culture of a friendly people, despite its idolatrous character, might have been looked at more sympathetically than when the same culture was that of an enemy people.

What might not Philo's report of his mission to Rome have been if he had had an audience with a Marcus Aurelius instead of with Caligula.[n] Suppose the Jewish philosopher had heard the Roman Emperor declare himself against limiting Roman citizenship to Romans or had heard him say that he, as the particular Marcus Aurelius, was a Roman citizen, but that as a man he was a citizen of the world-state.[o] One of the Greeks, whose name I do not recall, said

---

[m] Generally speaking the Justice was right. It should be added, however, that the Rabbis looked critically at Alexander, as did Diogenes, and that the Jews of Palestine did not forgive Caesar for having made Antipater procurator of their country.

[n] The Justice had in mind the delegation which the Jews of Alexandria sent to Caligula in the year 40 c.e., of which delegation Philo was a member.

[o] I mentioned the various reports in rabbinic literature of conversations or disputations between the Rabbis and distinguished pagans, such as those of R. Joshua b. Hananiah and Hadrian, R. Akiba and Tinius Rufus. I dwelt particularly on the report of the friendly personal relations between a Roman emperor Antoninus, who has been variously identified as Marcus Aurelius, Septimius Severus, Caracalla, and Lucius Verus, with a Rabbi who in turn has been identified with Rabbi Judah the Prince I and R. Judah the Prince II. The Justice, to my surprise, asked me whether the reports were legendary. I answered that that was the general opinion of scholars. He then wished to know whether in those tales the Rabbis got the better of the pagans. To which I replied that that was the case, so much so that Antoninus, for example, first erects an altar to God, shows the Jews great kindliness, and in the end becomes a true proselyte. The Justice remained silent for a time, and then added, "It is clear that

of Athens that she had "distanced the rest of mankind in thought and in speech, that her pupils [had] become the teachers of the rest of the world; and she has brought it about that the name 'Hellenes' suggests no longer a race but an intelligence, and that the title 'Hellenes' is applied rather to those who share our culture than those who share a common blood." [p]

I ask what effect would these sentiments have made on the Jewish sages? Would they have disregarded them and still boasted of the superior intelligence of the Jewish children of Palestine to the wise men of Athens? [q]

Well, we need not speculate as to what they might have done. But we know what we cannot, must not, and I am certain do not wish to do. We cannot today pin the hopes of humanity on any one particular people. We cannot today single out any one particular people as being virtuous, wise, and destined for greater things than all the rest. It would seem to me that even the strictest adherents of the Jewish faith ought to inquire whether their belief respecting the election of Israel is not perhaps based on a misinterpretation of revelation, or that there was a time limit to the belief. Maybe it was to be maintained until the world had rid itself of polytheism.

I should think it presumptuous for any people in this century to assert that it alone had a mission for all peoples, but that none of the other peoples had any mission for it. Every

---

if the Greeks and Romans had been favorably disposed toward the Jews and there had been understanding and sympathy on both sides, the Rabbis would have recognized the immense contributions those two peoples made to the advancement of civilization, and might not perhaps have rejected the possibility of their having been 'chosen' in some way."

[p] This quotation, from Isocrates' *Panegyricus*, was abbreviated by the Justice. I give it here in full in President Norlin's translation.

[q] I had mentioned earlier that there were many tales about the elders or wise men of Athens in rabbinic writings and that in not a few of those tales the Athenians are outwitted by Jewish children.

people, it is becoming more and more evident, has its own character. And insofar as it has a character of its own it has a mission. For it has that elusive something, its essence, which the other peoples do not have and of which they may stand in need. But all other peoples also have those elusive somethings, of some of which the Jewish people certainly stand in need. In the realm of things material one people may be a solitary benefactor and not a beneficiary. In the realm of the spirit there is no such solitary philanthropist. Here all peoples give and take, some more and some less, each giving what it has, and if it is wise it takes what it needs.

The experience of the Jewish people is unique. It is Jewish. Consequently the Jews have much to contribute toward the solution of the problems that perplex and confound all men. As a comparatively small people the Jewish people may be in a position to do better than bigger peoples. Palestine, when the Jews constitute the majority there, may, because of its very smallness, serve as a laboratory for some far-reaching experiments in democracy and social justice. But let us not forget that there are other small peoples who have in recent decades performed miracles in soil reclamation, in the rebuilding of their lands and peoples, and in advancing popular education and democratic ideals. Nor can we as Americans forget what our country has already done for the world and what it may yet do. The Pilgrim Fathers, in their day, and many of our most representative men since then, all conceived of America as God's gift to humanity. President Wilson spoke with deep conviction of America's mission. Perhaps Mr. Wilson had learned to speak this way because he was a constant reader of the Bible. Well then, let us teach all peoples that they are all chosen, and that each has a mission for all. I should prefer such an effort to that of boasting of our election.

CHURCH AND DEMOCRACY

Democracy in any sphere is a serious undertaking. It substitutes self-restraint for external restraint. It is more difficult to maintain than to achieve. It demands continuous sacrifice by the individual and more exigent obedience to the moral law than any other form of government. Success in any democratic undertaking must proceed from the individual. It is possible only where the process of perfecting the individual is pursued. His development is attained mainly in the processes of common living. Hence the industrial struggle is essentially an affair of the Church and is its imperative task.

BENJAMIN V. COHEN

On questions of international law consult Ben Cohen. If he cannot give you the answers they are probably not available.

COLLECTIVE BARGAINING

Since the adoption of the federal constitution, and notably within the last fifty years, we have passed through an economic and social revolution which affected the life of the people more fundamentally than any political revolution known to history. Widespread substitution of machinery for hand labor (thus multiplying a hundredfold man's productivity), and the annihilation of space through steam and electricity, have wrought changes in the conditions of life which are in many respects greater than those which had occurred in civilized countries during thousands of years preceding. The end was put to legalized human slavery—an institution which had existed since the dawn of history. But of vastly greater influence upon the lives of the great majority of all civilized peoples was the possibility which invention and discovery created of emancipating women and of liberating men called free from the excessive toil theretofore required to secure food, clothing and shelter. Yet, while invention and discovery created the possibility of releasing men and women from the thralldom of drudgery, there actually came, with the introduction of the factory system and the development of the business corporation, new dangers to liberty. Large publicly owned corporations replaced small privately owned concerns. Ownership of the instruments of production passed from the workman to the employer. Individual personal relations between the proprietor and his help ceased. The individual contract of service lost its character, because of the inequality in position between employer and employee. The group relation of employee to employer with collective bargaining became common, for it was essential to the workers' protection.

*

[70] It is almost inconceivable to my mind that a corporation with powers so concentrated as the Steel Corporation could get to a point where it would be willing to treat with the employees on equal terms. And unless they treat on equal terms then there is no such thing as democratization. The treatment on equal terms with them involves not merely the making of a contract; it must develop into a continuing relation. The making of a contract with a union is a long step. It is collective bargaining—a great advance. But it is only the first step. In order that collective bargaining should result in industrial democracy it must go further and create practically an industrial government—a relation between employer and employee where the problems as they arise from day to day, or from month to month, or from year to year, may come up for consideration and solution as they come up in our political government.

In that way conditions are created best adapted to securing proper consideration of any question arising. The representative of each party is heard—and strives to advance the

interest he represents. It is the conflict of these opposing
forces which produces the contract ultimately. But adequately to solve the trade problems there must be some
machinery which will deal with these problems as they arise
from day to day. You must create something akin to a government of the trade before you reach a real approach to
democratization. You must create a relation of employer
and employee similar to that which exists in the trade under
the protocol with the preferential union shop.[37]

*

The question here is not so much the question whether
the number of cents per hour that this miserable creature
receives is a little more or a little less. Whether it is enough,
none of us are competent to determine. What we are competent to determine, sitting right here, as American citizens,
is whether any men in the United States, be they directors
of the Steel Corporation or anyone else, are entitled and
can safely determine the conditions under which a large
portion of the American [workmen] shall live; whether it is
not absolutely essential to fairness, for results in an American democracy, to say that the great mass of working people
should have an opportunity to combine, and by their collective bargaining secure for themselves what may be a fair
return for their labor. There is the fundamental question,
and there is the question which is at the bottom of this situation. The denial of that right of collective bargaining is an
explanation of the miserable condition of the workingmen
in the steel industry.

COMMON PEOPLE

This investigation [Ballinger Case] has been referred to as
a struggle for conservation, a struggle against the special interests. It is that: but it is far more. In its essence, it is the

[37] See also Employer and Employee.

struggle for democracy, the struggle of the small man against the overpowering influence of the big; politically as well as financially, the struggle to establish the right of every American to equal justice in the public service as well as in the courts, that no official is so highly stationed that he may trample ruthlessly and unjustly upon even the humblest American citizen. The cause of Glavis is the cause of the common people, and more especially the cause of the hundreds of thousands of government officials.

COMPETITION [38]

Undoubtedly competition involves waste. What human activity does not? The wastes of democracy are among the greatest obvious wastes, but we have compensations in democracy which far outweigh that waste and make it more efficient than absolutism. So it is with competition. The waste is relatively insignificant.[39] There are wastes of competition which do not develop, but kill. These the law can and should eliminate, by regulating competition.

*

The history of combinations has shown that what one may do with impunity, may have intolerable results when done by several in cooperation. Similarly what approximately equal individual traders may do in honorable rivalry may result in grave injustice and public injury, if done by a great corporation in a particular field of business which it is able to dominate. In other words, a method of competition fair among equals may be very unfair if applied where there is inequality of resources.

*

[75] Unrestricted competition, with its abuses and excesses, leads to monopoly, because these abuses and excesses

---

[38] See also Regulated Competition, Sherman Law.
[39] Repeated under Democracy.

prevent competition from functioning properly as a regulator of business. Competition proper is beneficent, because it acts as an incentive to the securing of better quality or lower cost. It operates also as a repressive of greed, keeping within bounds the natural inclination to exact the largest profit obtainable. Unfair and oppressive competition defeats those purposes. It prevents the natural development which should attend rivalry and which gives success to those who contribute most to the community by their development of their own business and the exercise of moderation in the exaction of profits. It substitutes devious and corrupt methods for honest rivalry and seeks to win, not by superior methods, but by force. Its purpose is not to excel, but to destroy.

*

Some people believe that the existing conditions threaten even the stability of the capitalistic system. Economists are searching for the causes of this disorder and are re-examining the basis of our industrial structure. Most of them realize that failure to distribute widely the profits of industry has been a prime cause of our present plight. But rightly or wrongly, many persons think that one of the major contributing causes has been unbridled competition.

*

No system of regulation can safely be substituted for the operation of individual liberty as expressed in competition. It would be like attempting to substitute a regulated monarchy for a republic.

*

It seems self-evident not only when you consider the different forms of methods of transportation, like railroad as against water-carrier or railroad as against trolley, but it is equally self-evident when you are considering what ought to be the competition between the different members or concerns in the same class. The one that can do it the best—and usually that means the one that can do it the cheapest—ought to perform the service.

COMPETITION FROM WITHIN

Every business requires for its business health the *memento mori* of competition from without. It requires likewise a certain competition from within, which can exist only where the ownership and management, on the one hand, and the employees, on the other, shall each be alert, hopeful, self-respecting, and free to work out for themselves the best conceivable conditions.

CONCENTRATION

[80] I doubt whether anybody who is himself engaged in any important business has time to be a director in more than one large corporation. If he seeks to know about the affairs of that one corporation as much as he should know, not only in the interest of the stockholders, but in the interest of the community, he will have a field for study that will certainly occupy all the time that he has.[40]

CONCRETE PROBLEMS

As a whole I have not got as much from books as I have from tackling concrete problems. I have generally run up against a problem, have painfully tried to think it out, with a measure of success, and have then read a book and found to my surprise that some other chap was before me.

CONSERVATION

Conservation, in its very essence, is preserving things public for the people, preserving them so that the people may have them. To accomplish this is the aim of our Republic. It is the aim of our great democracy that men shall, so far

---

[40] Repeated under Monopoly.

as humanly possible, have equal opportunities, and that the differences in opportunities to which men have been subject elsewhere shall not prevail here.[41]

CONSERVATISM

True conservatism involves progress. . . . Unless our financial leaders are capable of progress, the institutions which they are trying to conserve will lose their foundation.

CONSTITUTION

The federal constitution . . . perhaps the greatest of human experiments.[42]

CONTROL AND COOPERATION

[85] The citizen in a successful democracy must not only have education, he must be free. Men are not free if dependent industrially upon the arbitrary will of another. Industrial liberty on the part of the worker cannot, therefore, exist if there be overweening industrial power. Some curb must be placed upon capitalistic combination. Nor will even this curb be effective unless the workers cooperate, as in trade unions. Control and cooperation are both essential to industrial liberty.

COOPERATIVE MOVEMENT

Farmers, workingmen, and clerks are learning to use their little capital and their savings to help one another instead of turning over their money to the great bankers for safekeeping, and to be themselves exploited. And may we not expect that when the cooperative movement develops in America, merchants and manufacturers will learn from farmers and workingmen how to help themselves by helping one another, and thus join in attaining the New Freedom for all? When merchants and manufacturers learn this lesson,

---

[41] See also American Ideals.
[42] Repeated under Experimentation.

money kings will lose subjects, and swollen fortunes may shrink; but industries will flourish, because the faculties of men will be liberated and developed.

CORPORATION LAWYER

Instead of holding a position of independence, between the wealthy and the people, prepared to curb the excesses of either, able lawyers have, to a large extent, allowed themselves to become adjuncts of great corporations and have neglected the obligation to use their powers for the protection of the people. We hear much of the "corporation lawyer," and far too little of the "people's lawyer." The great opportunity of the American Bar is and will be to stand again as it did in the past, ready to protect also the interests of the people.[43]

COURTS AND THE PEOPLE

I believe that the courts and the people have been too far apart. There is no subject so complex that the people cannot be interested in it and made to see the truth about it if pains enough be taken; and I believe that a common agreement of public sentiment should influence the court's decision on many a question.

CUTTHROAT COMPETITION

Monopoly is the natural outcome of cutthroat competition.

DANGERS TO DEMOCRACY

[90] Many dangers to democracy . . . are inherent in these huge aggregations.[44]

DECEPTION

The breaches of trust committed or permitted by men of high financial reputation, the disclosure of the payment of

---

[43] See also Lawyers' Education, Legal Profession.
[44] Repeated under Monopoly.

exorbitant salaries and commissions, the illegal participation
in syndicate profits, the persistent perversion of sacred trust
funds to political purposes, the cooperation of the large
New York companies to control the legislatures of the country—these disclosures are indeed distressing; but the practice
of deliberate and persistent deception of the public which
the testimony discloses, though less dramatic, is even more
serious. Talleyrand said, "Language was made to conceal
thought." George W. Perkins would teach us that "Book-
keeping was made to conceal facts."

DELICATE OPERATION

To exercise a sound judgment in the difficult affairs of
business is, at best, a delicate operation. And no man can
successfully perform that function whose mind is diverted,
however innocently, from the study of: "What is best in the
long run for the company of which I am a director?"

DEMAND

Many labor leaders have regarded demand as static, as
something fixed. They have therefore assumed that if there
is a hundred per cent to divide, it will last longer if we each
do less, and it will go further. That I believe to be absolutely
unsound, as shown by experience. There is no fixed demand.
Demand is capable of almost any degree of expansion. It is
partly this unfortunate lack of confidence in employers, as
a whole, and partly a failure to recognize the results of economic experience, to which the tendency of many labor
leaders to restrict production by the individual worker is
due.

LEWIS N. DEMBITZ

To those of my generation, your father [Lewis N. Dem-
bitz] was a living university. With him, life was unending
intellectual ferment. He grappled eagerly with the most difficult problems in mathematics and the sciences, in eco-

nomics, government and politics. In the diversity of his intellectual interests, in his longing to discover truths, in his pleasure in argumentation and the process of thinking, he reminded one of the Athenians. He loved books as a vehicle of knowledge and an inciter to thought; he made his love contagious.

It is appropriate that his influence should be remembered in the library where he would have worked, and is in part the fruit of his influence. A collection of books is the memorial for which he would have cared most. And the collection which tells of Palestine's rebirth seems the most appropriate. For the deepest of his studies were those allied to the Jewish religion. He was orthodox. He observed the law. But, he was not satisfied with merely observing it. He sought to understand the law in order to find its reason; he studied deeply into the history of the Jewish people. His was not the drive of intellectual curiosity into the realm of dead knowledge. He recognized in the past the mirror of the future; a future which would be a noble and glorious one for his people. It was natural that he should have been among the first in America to support Herzl in his effort to build a new Palestine.

DEMOCRACY

[95] Democracy means not merely, I had almost said not so much, the rights of the whole people, as the duties of the whole people.

*

We need democracy at all times no matter what the system is under which we work.

*

The wastes of democracy are among the greatest obvious wastes, but we have compensations in democracy which far outweigh that waste, and make it more efficient than absolutism. So it is with competition. Incentive and development which are incident to the freer system of business result in so much greater achievement that the waste is relatively insignificant.[45] The margin between that which men naturally do, and that which they can do, is so great that a system which urges men on to action and develops individual enterprise and initiative is preferable, in spite of the wastes that necessarily attend that process.

DEMOCRACY AND ARISTOCRACY

Democracy rests upon two pillars; one, the principle that all men are equally entitled to life, liberty and the pursuit of happiness; and the other, the conviction that such equal opportunity will most advance civilization. Aristocracy, on the other hand, denies both these postulates. It rests upon the principle of the superman. It willingly subordinates the many to the few, and seeks to justify sacrificing the individual by insisting that civilization will be advanced by such sacrifices.[46]

DEMOCRATIC IDEALS

Democratic ideals cannot be attained by the mentally undeveloped. In a government where every one is part sovereign, every one should be competent, if not to govern at least to understand the problems of government; and to this end education is an essential.[47]

*

[100] Democratic ideals can be attained only where those who govern exercise their power not by alleged divine right or inheritance, but by force of character and intelligence.[48]

---

[45] See Competition.
[46] See also Educational Standard, Education of Electorate.
[47] Repeated under Jews and Democracy.
[48] Repeated under Character and Intelligence, Jews and Democracy.

*

Our great beneficent experiment in democracy will fail unless the people, our rulers, are developed in character and intelligence.[49]

DEMOCRATIC METHODS

Democratic methods are necessarily slow and often seem unreasonable. And the fact that our instruments are man with his weaknesses and defects, is at times exasperating.

DEPRECIATION

There is no regularity in the development of depreciation. It does not proceed in accordance with any mathematical law. There is nothing in business experience or in the training of experts, which enables man to say to what extent service life will be impaired by the operations of a single year, or of a series of years less than the service life.

DESPOTISM

There is no way in which to safeguard people from despotism except to prevent despotism.[50]

*

[105] Despotism, be it financial or political, is vulnerable, unless it is believed to rest upon a moral sanction.[51]

DIFFERENTIATION NOT UNIFORMITY

In differentiation, not in uniformity, lies the path of progress.[52]

---

[49] Repeated under Leisure.
[50] Repeated under Monopoly.
[51] See Bankers' Ethics.
[52] See America.

WILLIAM O. DOUGLAS

Justice Douglas will leave his mark on the Court. I am very much pleased with my successor. He would have been my own choice.[53]

DUTIES

The greatest progress will perhaps be made if all of you can give larger thought to your duties than to your rights.

DUTY

Duty must be accepted as the dominant conception in life.

DUTY TO THE COMMUNITY

[110] All rights are derived from the purposes of the society in which they exist; above all rights rises duty to the community.

EARLY NEW ENGLANDERS

The early New Englanders appreciated fully that education is an essential of potential equality. The founding of their common school system was coincident with the founding of the colonies; and even the establishment of institutions for higher education did not lag far behind. Harvard College was founded but six years after the first settlement of Boston.[54]

EDUCATED JEW

The educated descendants of a people which in its infancy cast aside the Golden Calf and put its faith in the invisible God cannot worthily in its maturity worship worldly distinction and things material.

---

[53] I am not sure about the last sentence. The Justice may have said "No other appointee or successor would have pleased me as much."
[54] Repeated under Jews and Democracy.

EDUCATION

Education must continue throughout life.

EDUCATIONAL ENDOWMENTS

I have, and I think many must have, a grave apprehension as to some of the great educational endowments of the so-called private universities in contrast with the State universities. I think we are fortunate in having in this country both the one and the other; and that other foundations, if they are not too large, may be very beneficial; provided always that there are other forces in governmental agencies which can counteract them. Still I cannot help feeling a certain apprehension as to later results of these foundations.

EDUCATIONAL STANDARD[55]

[115] The intellectual development of citizens may not be allowed to end at fourteen. With most people whose minds have really developed, the age of fourteen is rather the beginning than the end of the educational period. The educational standard required of a democracy is obviously high. The citizen should be able to comprehend among other things the many great and difficult problems of industry, commerce and finance, which with us necessarily become political questions. He must learn about men as well as things.

EDUCATION OF ELECTORATE[55]

I am unwavering in my belief in democracy of the old representative type, when the representative was to exercise his judgment and discretion and not merely voice the will of the electorate. The trouble with our democracy is that we have not been willing to pay the price—that is, educate the electorate. That must be a continuous process—not a quadrennial or annual campaign. And it must involve a much wider participation in government. I think consider-

---

[55] See also Democracy and Aristocracy.

ation of governmental problems can be made for a large
section of the people the most alluring of occupations. And
there will be time for this when we have the five-day week
and six-hour day.

EFFICIENCY[56]

Efficiency and economy imply employment of the right
instrument and material as well as their use in the right
manner. To use a machine, after a much better and more
economical one has become available, is as inefficient as
to use two men to operate an efficient machine when the
work could be performed equally well by one at half the
labor cost.

*

The world's demand for efficiency is so great and the
supply so small, that the price of efficiency is high in every
field of human activity.

*

While a business may be too small to be efficient, efficiency does not grow indefinitely with increasing size. There
is in every line of business a unit of greatest efficiency. What
the size of that unit is cannot be determined in advance by
a general rule. It will vary in different lines of business and
with different concerns in the same line. It will vary with the
same concern at different times because of different conditions. What the most efficient size is can be learned definitely only by experience. The unit of greatest efficiency is
reached when the disadvantages of size counterbalance the
advantages. The unit of greatest efficiency is exceeded when
the disadvantages of size outweigh the advantages. For a
unit of business may be too large to be efficient as well as

---

[56] See also Interlocking Directorates, Monopoly and Efficiency,
Scientific Management.

too small. And in no American industry is monopoly an essential condition of the greatest efficiency.

*

[120] Real efficiency in any business in which conditions are ever changing must ultimately depend, in large measure, upon the correctness of the judgment exercised, almost from day to day, on the important problems as they arise.

EFFICIENCY AND SOCIAL IDEALS

Efficiency is the hope of democracy. Efficiency means greater production with less effort and at less cost, through the elimination of unnecessary waste, human and material. How else can we hope to attain our social ideals?

The "right to life" guaranteed by our Constitution is now being interpreted according to demands of social justice and of democracy as the right to *live*, and not merely to exist. In order to live men must have the opportunity of developing their faculties; and they must live under conditions in which their faculties may develop naturally and healthily.

In the first place, there must be abolition of child labor, shorter hours of labor, and regular days of rest, so that men and women may conserve health, may fit themselves to be citizens of a free country, and may perform their duties as citizens. In other words, men and women must have leisure, which the Athenians called "freedom" or liberty. In the second place, the earnings of men and women must be greater, so that they may live under conditions conducive to health and to mental and moral development.

Our American ideals cannot be attained unless an end is put to the misery due to poverty.[57]

These demands for shorter working time, for higher earnings and for better conditions cannot conceivably be met unless the productivity of man is increased. No mere re-

[57] See American Ideals.

distribution of the profits of industry could greatly improve the condition of the working classes. Indeed, the principal gain that can be expected from any such redistribution of profits is that it may remove the existing sense of injustice and discontent, which are the greatest obstacles to efficiency.

EFFICIENCY'S TEST

The real test of efficiency comes when success has to be struggled for.

ELIMINATION OF WASTE

I believe all intelligent and enlightened thinkers will recognize, that the only way permanently and appreciably to better the condition of labor, is to increase productivity and to eliminate the waste. That is what scientific management is. It means merely getting more with less effort. It means stopping all waste effort either in the exertion of the individuals or in goods. Just how you are going to apply the principle is a matter of detail. It is most important that it shall be applied democratically. It cannot be successfully applied otherwise in the long run; that is, both employer and employee must come to recognize the fact that the elimination of waste is beneficial to both sides and that they must cooperate to produce the best results and the most effective methods of production.[58]

EMERSON

I have been indulging in Emerson also—and can conscientiously say that my admiration for him is on the increase. I have read a few sentences of his, which are alone enough to make the man immortal.

EMPLOYER AND EMPLOYEE[59]

[125] Don't assume that the interests of employer and employee are necessarily hostile—that what is good for one

---

[58] Repeated under Employer and Employee.
[59] See also Collective Bargaining, Unrestricted Power.

is necessarily bad for the other. The opposite is more apt
to be the case. While they have different interests, they are
likely to prosper or suffer together.

*

Both labor and employers should bear constantly in mind
that each is his brother's keeper; that every employer is
injured by any single employer who does labor a wrong;
and that every laboring man and every union is injured by
every individual unionist who does an employer wrong. The
influence of a single wrongful act by one who can be classi-
fied, is tremendous. It affects every other member of the
class. When an employer acts improperly toward his employees, it is the business of other employers to see that
such conduct is prevented, for his wrong will injure them.
And in the same way any lack of fairness and any act of
lawlessness on the part of labor is certain to injure other
workers and the unions as a whole, and the individual members of labor unions with employers.[60]

*

Our employers can no more afford to be absolute masters
of their employees than they could afford to submit to the
mastery of their employees.[61]

*

Nine-tenths of the serious controversies which arise in life
result from misunderstanding, result from one man not
knowing the facts which to the other man seem important,
or otherwise failing to appreciate his point of view. A properly conducted conference involves a frank disclosure of
such facts—patient, careful argument, willingness to listen
and to consider.[62]

[60] See also Unions.
[61] Repeated under Industrial Democracy.
[62] Repeated under Proper Conferences, Serious Controversies.

Bluff and bluster have no place there. The spirit must be, "Come, let us reason together." Such a conference is impossible where the employer clings to the archaic belief commonly expressed in the words, "This is my business, and I will run it as I please." It is impossible where the labor representative, swaggering in his power to inflict injury by strike and boycott, is seeking an unfair advantage of the employers, or would seek to maintain even a proper position by improper means. Such conferences will succeed only if employer and employee recognize that, even if there be no so-called system of profit-sharing, they are in a most important sense partners, and that each is entitled to a patient hearing, with a mind as open as the prejudice of self-interest permits.[63]

*

Employer and employee must come to recognize the fact that the elimination of waste is beneficial to both sides and that they must cooperate to produce the best results and the most effective methods of production.[64]

EMPLOYERS AND UNIONS

[130] The employers' refusal to deal with a union is ordinarily due to erroneous reasoning or false sentiment. The man who refuses to deal with the union acts ordinarily from a good motive. He is impressed with "union dictation." He is apt to think "this is my business and the American has the right of liberty of contract." He honestly believes that he is standing up for a high principle and is willing often to run the risk of having his business ruined rather than abandon that principle. They have not thought out clearly enough that liberty means exercising one's rights consistently with a like exercise of rights by other people; that liberty is distinguished from license in that it is subject to

[63] Repeated under Proper Conferences.
[64] See Elimination of Waste.

certain restrictions and that no one can expect to secure liberty in the sense in which we recognize it in America without having his rights curtailed in those respects in which it is necessary to limit them in the general public interest.[65] The failure of many employers to recognize these simple truths is a potent reason why employers have not been willing to deal with unions. I think our employers, as a rule, are kind-hearted; they mean to do right; they mean to be just; and there is no difference between the men who have fought the hardest against labor unions and those who have yielded to and dealt with labor unions in that respect, except that the former have not had that education which comes from actual active cooperation with unions in the solution of these problems.[66]

*

I should say to those employers who stand for the open shop, that they ought to recognize that it is for their interests as well as that of the community that unions should be powerful and responsible; that it is to their interests to build up the unions, to aid as far as they can in making them stronger, and to create conditions under which the unions shall be led by the ablest and most experienced men. A large part of all union activity today, and in the past, has been devoted to the struggle for existence; and that fact accounts also for a large part of union excesses. As nearly as possible union existence should be assured so that the efforts of the leaders might be devoted to solving the fundamental and difficult problems of discipline and organization, and the working out of other problems of the trades.[67]

ENGLAND

England is nearer civilization than any other country. That it is nearer democracy seems clear. As I watch events

---

[65] Repeated under Liberty.   [66] See also Unions.   [67] See also Unions.

from day to day I am ever more impressed with the existence of a potent public opinion—expressing itself manfully and with much immediate effect. Our own machinery—referendum, initiative, primary elections, and elective officials galore—is a miserable substitute for the alert, intelligent watchfulness which is reflected generally in the press and which finds, in the interrogations in the House of Commons and in letters to the *Times*, the means of uncovering wrong action before it has become irremediable or has ceased to be of moment.

ENLIGHTENED UNSELFISHNESS

We ought to develop enlightened unselfishness, as a substitute for the old so-called enlightened selfishness; and enlightened unselfishness would give us all a great deal more than we have.

E PLURIBUS UNUM

E pluribus unum—Out of many one—was the motto adopted by the founders of the Republic when they formed a union of the thirteen states. To these we have added, from time to time, thirty-five more. The founders were convinced, as we are, that a strong nation could be built through federation. They were also convinced, as we are, that in America, under a free government, many peoples would make one nation. Throughout all these years we have admitted to our country and to citizenship immigrants from the diverse lands of Europe. We had faith that thereby we would best serve ourselves and mankind. This faith has been justified. The United States has grown great. The immigrants and their immediate descendants have proved themselves as loyal as any citizens of the country. Liberty has knit us closely together as Americans.[68] Note the common devotion to our country's emblem expressed at the recent

---

[68] Repeated under Liberty.

Flag Day celebration in New York by boys and girls representing more than twenty different nationalities warring abroad.

EQUALITY OF OPPORTUNITY

[135] I have many opinions, but I am not a doctrinaire. My habit of mind has been to move from one problem to another, giving to each, while it is before me, my undivided study. I am a Democrat, but I have laid most stress on the little 'd.' Give me a free field. Provide equality of opportunity and we attain the New Freedom.[69]

EXCESSES

Excesses of competition lead to monopoly, as excesses of liberty lead to absolutism. The extremes meet.[70]

EXCESSES OF CAPITAL

The greatest factors making for communism, socialism, or anarchy among a free people are the excesses of capital; because, as Lincoln said of slavery, "Every drop of blood drawn with the lash shall be requited by another drawn with the sword." It is certain that among a free people every excess of capital must in time be repaid by the excessive demands of those who have not the capital. Every act of injustice on the part of the rich will be met by another act or many acts of injustice on the part of the people.[71]

*

The immense corporate wealth will necessarily develop a hostility from which much trouble will come to us unless the excesses of capital are curbed, through the respect for law, as the excesses of democracy were curbed seventy-five years ago.[72]

---

[69] Repeated under New Freedom.
[70] Repeated under Regulated Competition.
[71] Repeated under People and Rich.
[72] Repeated under Legal Profession.

EXISTING INSTITUTIONS

Seek for betterment within the broad lines of existing institutions. Do so by attacking evil *in situ;* and proceed from the individual to the general. Remember that progress is necessarily slow; that remedies are necessarily tentative; that because of varying conditions there must be much and constant enquiry into facts . . . and much experimentation; and that always and everywhere the intellectual, moral and spiritual development of those concerned will remain an essential—and the main factor—in real betterment.[73]

This development of the individual is, thus, both a necessary means and the end sought. For our objective is the making of men and women who shall be free, self-respecting members of a democracy—and who shall be worthy of respect. Improvement in material conditions of the worker and ease are the incidents of better conditions—valuable mainly as they may ever increase opportunities for development.

EXPERIMENTATION[74]

[140] The people of the United States are now confronted with an emergency more serious than war. Misery is widespread, in a time, not of scarcity, but of overabundance. The long-continued depression has brought unprecedented unemployment, a catastrophic fall in commodity prices, and a volume of economic losses which threatens our financial institutions. Some people believe that the existing conditions threaten even the stability of the capitalistic system. Economists are searching for the causes of this disorder and are re-examining the basis of our industrial structure. Business men are seeking possible remedies. Most of them realize that failure to distribute widely the profits of industry has been a prime cause of our present plight. But, rightly or

[73] Repeated under Main Factor in Social Betterment.
[74] See also United States Supreme Court.

wrongly, many persons think that one of the major contributing causes has been unbridled competition. Increasingly, doubt is expressed whether it is economically wise, or morally right, that men should be permitted to add to the producing facilities of an industry which is already suffering from overcapacity. In justification of that doubt, men point to the excess capacity of our productive facilities resulting from their vast expansion without corresponding increase in the consumptive capacity of the people. They assert that through improved methods of manufacture, made possible by advances in science and invention and vast accumulation of capital, our industries had become capable of producing from 30 to 100 per cent more than was consumed even in days of vaunted prosperity; and that the present capacity will, for a long time, exceed the needs of business. All agree that irregularity in employment—the greatest of our evils—cannot be overcome unless production and consumption are more nearly balanced.[75] Many insist there must be some form of economic control. There are plans for proration. There are many proposals for stabilization. And some thoughtful men of wide business experience insist that all projects for stabilization and proration must prove futile unless, in some way, the equivalent of the certificate of public convenience and necessity is made a prerequisite to embarking new capital in an industry in which the capacity already exceeds the production schedules.

Whether that view is sound nobody knows. The objections to the proposal are obvious and grave. The remedy might bring evils worse than the present disease. The obstacles to success seem insuperable. The economic and social sciences are largely uncharted seas.[76] We have been none too successful in the modest essays in economic control already entered upon. The new proposal involves a vast

---

[75] Repeated under Irregularity of Employment.
[76] Repeated under Uncharted Seas.

extension of the area of control. Merely to acquire the
knowledge essential as a basis for the exercise of this multitude of judgments would be a formidable task; and each
of the thousands of these judgments would call for some
measure of prophecy. Even more serious are the obstacles
to success inherent in the demands which execution of the
project would make upon human intelligence and upon the
character of men. Man is weak and his judgment is at best
fallible.[77]

Yet the advances in the exact sciences and the achievements in invention remind us that the seemingly impossible
sometimes happens. There are many men now living who
were in the habit of using the age-old expression: "It is as
impossible as flying." The discoveries in physical science,
the triumphs in invention, attest the value of the process of
trial and error.[78] In large measure, these advances have been
due to experimentation. In those fields experimentation has,
for two centuries, been not only free but encouraged. Some
people assert that our present plight is due, in part, to the
limitations set by courts upon experimentation in the fields
of social and economic science; and to the discouragement
to which proposals for betterment there have been subjected
otherwise. There must be power in the States and the nation
to remold, through experimentation, our economic practices and institutions to meet changing social and economic
needs. I cannot believe that the framers of the Fourteenth
Amendment, or the states which ratified it, intended to
deprive us of the power to correct the evils of technological
unemployment and excess productive capacity which have
attended progress in the useful arts.

To stay experimentation in things social and economic
is a grave responsibility. Denial of the right to experiment
may be fraught with serious consequences to the nation. It

[77] Repeated under Man.
[78] Repeated under Trial and Error.

is one of the happy incidents of the federal system that a single courageous state may, if its citizens choose, serve as a laboratory; and try novel social and economic experiments without risk to the rest of the country. This Court has the power to prevent an experiment. We may strike down the statute which embodies it on the ground that, in our opinion, the measure is arbitrary, capricious, or unreasonable. We have power to do this, because the due process clause has been held by the Court applicable to matters of substantive law as well as to matters of procedure. But, in the exercise of this high power, we must be ever on our guard, lest we erect our prejudices into legal principles. If we would guide by the light of reason, we must let our minds be bold.[79]

*

Our social and industrial welfare demands that ample scope should be given for social as well as mechanical invention. It is a condition not only of progress but of conserving that which we have. Nothing could be more revolutionary than to close the door to social experimentation. The whole subject of woman's entry into industry is an experiment. And surely the federal constitution—itself perhaps the greatest of human experiments [80]—does not prohibit such modest attempts as the woman's minimum-wage act to reconcile the existing industrial system with our striving for social justice and the preservation of the race.

FACTS [81]

Whether a measure relating to the public welfare is arbitrary or unreasonable, whether it has no substantial relation to the end proposed, is obviously not to be determined by assumptions or by *a priori* reasoning. The judgment should

[79] See Boldness.
[80] See Constitution.
[81] See also Logic of Realities.

be based upon a consideration of relevant facts, actual or possible—*Ex facto jus oritur*. That ancient rule must prevail in order that we may have a system of living law.[82]

*

The difficulty in deciding any question that comes up is really the difficulty in getting at the facts.

*

What we must do in America is not to attack our judges, but to educate them. All judges should be made to feel, as many judges already do, that the things needed to protect liberty are radically different from what they were fifty years back. In some courts the judges' conceptions of their own powers must also change. Some judges have decided a law unconstitutional simply because they considered the law unwise. These judges should be made to feel that they have no such right, that their business is not to decide whether the view taken by the legislature is a wise view, but whether a body of men could reasonably hold such a view. In the past the courts have reached their conclusions largely deductively from preconceived notions and precedents. The method I have tried to employ in arguing cases before them has been inductive, reasoning from the facts.[83]

FAILURE OF LIFE INSURANCE COMPANIES

[145] The causes of failure of life insurance companies have been excessive expense, unsound investment, or dishonest management.

FALSIFICATION OF BOOKS

In the case of common criminals flight is accepted as confession of guilt. With financiers and business men falsification of books has hitherto been considered the strongest

---

[82] See also Lawyers' Training.
[83] Repeated under Judges.

evidence of guilt. Yet the falsification of the books of these companies has been a persistent practice. Secret ledgers have been opened in which were entered questionable investments and more questionable expenditures. Hundreds of thousands spent "for legislative purposes" were charged up in real estate accounts. So elaborate has been the system of fraudulent entries that after months of investigation the particular form of rascality embodied in the Equitable's $685,000 Mercantile Trust Company, so-called "yellow-dog," account has not yet been detected.

FEAR, REPRESSION, HATE

Fear breeds repression . . . repression breeds hate . . . hate menaces stable government.[84]

FINANCIAL DEPENDENCE

American democracy rests upon the basis of the free citizen.[85] We accord (to the men) universal suffrage. We urge strenuously upon every voter the duty of exercising this right. We insist that the voter should exercise it in the interest of others as well as of himself. We give thus to the citizen the rights of a free man. We impose upon him a duty that can be intrusted with safety only to free men. Politically, the American workingman is free—so far as law can make him so. But is he really free? Can any man be really free who is constantly in danger of becoming dependent for mere subsistence upon somebody and something else than his own exertion and conduct? Men are not free while financially dependent upon the will of other individuals. Financial dependence is consistent with freedom only where claim to support rests upon right, and not upon favor.[86]

---

[84] Repeated under Freedom of Speech.
[85] See American Democracy.
[86] See also Greatest Danger, Industrial Absolutism, Industrial Liberty.

FINANCIAL INDEPENDENCE [87]

There is no such thing as freedom for a man who under normal conditions is not financially free. We must therefore find means to create in the individual financial independence against sickness, accidents, unemployment, old age, and the dread of leaving his family destitute, if he suffer premature death. For we have become practically a world of employees; and, if a man is to have real freedom of contract in dealing with his employer, he must be financially independent of these ordinary contingencies. Unless we protect him from this oppression, it is foolish to call him free.

*

[150]   If the American is to be fitted for his task as ruler, he must have besides education and industrial liberty also some degree of financial independence. Our existing industrial system is converting an ever increasing percentage of the population into wage-earners; and experience teaches us that a large part of these become at some time financial dependents, by reason of sickness, accident, invalidity, superannuation, unemployment, or premature death of the bread-winner of the family. Contingencies like these, which are generally referred to in the individual case as misfortunes, are now recognized as ordinary incidents in the life of the wage-earner. The need of providing indemnity against financial losses from such ordinary contingencies in the workingman's life has become apparent and is already being supplied in other countries.

FREEDOM OF SPEECH

Those who won our independence believed that the final end of the State was to make men free to develop their faculties, and that in its government the deliberative forces

---

[87] See also Greatest Danger.

should prevail over the arbitrary. They valued liberty both as an end and as a means. They believed liberty to be the secret of happiness and courage to be the secret of liberty. They believed that freedom to think as you will and to speak as you think are means indispensable to the discovery and spread of political truth; that without free speech and assembly discussion would be futile; that with them, discussion affords ordinarily adequate protection against the dissemination of noxious doctrine; that the greatest menace to freedom is an inert people; [88] that public discussion is a political duty; and that this should be a fundamental principle of the American Government. They recognized the risks to which all human institutions are subject. But they knew that order cannot be secured merely through fear of punishment for its infraction; that it is hazardous to discourage thought, hope, and imagination; that fear breeds repression; that repression breeds hate; that hate menaces stable government; [89] that the path of safety lies in the opportunity to discuss freely supposed grievances and proposed remedies; and that the fitting remedy for evil counsels is good ones. Believing in the power of reason as applied through public discussion, they eschewed silence coerced by law—the argument of force in its worst form.[90] Recognizing the occasional tyrannies of governing majorities, they amended the Constitution so that free speech and assembly should be guaranteed.

Fear of serious injury cannot alone justify suppression of free speech and assembly. Men feared witches and burnt women. It is the function of speech to free men from the bondage of irrational fears.[91] To justify suppression of free speech there must be reasonable ground to fear that the

---

[88] Repeated under Greatest Menace to Freedom.
[89] See Fear, Repression, Hate.
[90] See Argument of Force.
[91] Repeated under Function of Speech.

serious evil will result if free speech is practiced. There must be reasonable ground to believe that the danger apprehended is imminent. There must be reasonable ground to believe that the evil to be prevented is a serious one. Every denunciation of existing law tends in some measure to increase the probability that there will be violation of it. Condonation of a breach enhances the probability. Expressions of approval add to the probability. Propagation of the criminal state of mind by teaching syndicalism increases it. Advocacy of law-breaking heightens it still further. But even advocacy of violation, however reprehensible morally, is not a justification for denying free speech where the advocacy falls short of incitement and there is nothing to indicate that the advocacy would be immediately acted on. The wide difference between advocacy and incitement, between preparation and attempt, between assembling and conspiracy, must be borne in mind. In order to support a finding of clear and present danger it must be shown either that immediate serious violence was to be expected or was advocated, or that the past conduct furnished reason to believe that such advocacy was then contemplated.

Those who won our independence by revolution were not cowards. They did not fear political change. They did not exalt order at the cost of liberty. To courageous, self-reliant men, with confidence in the power of free and fearless reasoning applied through the processes of popular government, no danger flowing from speech can be deemed clear and present, unless the incidence of the evil apprehended is so imminent that it may befall before there is opportunity for full discussion. If there be time to expose through discussion the falsehood and fallacies, to avert the evil by the processes of education, the remedy to be applied is more speech, not enforced silence. Only an emergency can justify repression. Such must be the rule if authority is to be reconciled with freedom. Such, in my opinion, is the command of the Constitution. It is therefore always open to Americans to challenge a law abridging free speech and assembly by showing that there was no emergency justifying it.

Moreover, even imminent danger cannot justify resort to prohibition of these functions essential to effective democracy, unless the evil apprehended is relatively serious. Prohibition of free speech and assembly is a measure so stringent that it would be inappropriate as the means for averting a relatively trivial harm to society. A police measure may be unconstitutional merely because the remedy, although effective as means of protection, is unduly harsh or oppressive. Thus, a State might, in the exercise of its police power, make any trespass upon the land of another a crime, regardless of the results or of the intent or purpose of the trespasser. It might, also, punish an attempt, a conspiracy, or an incitement to commit the trespass. But it is hardly conceivable that this Court would hold constitutional a statute which punished as a felony the mere voluntary assembly with a society formed to teach that pedestrians had the moral right to cross uninclosed, unposted, waste lands and to advocate their doing so, even if there was imminent danger that advocacy would lead to a trespass. The fact that speech is likely to result in some violence or in destruction of property is not enough to justify its suppression. There must be the probability of serious injury to the State. Among free men, the deterrents ordinarily to be applied to prevent crime are education and punishment for violations of the law, not abridgment of the rights of free speech and assembly.

*

The extent to which Congress may, under the Constitution, interfere with free speech, was . . . declared by a unanimous Court to be this:

"The question in every case is whether the words . . . are used in such circumstances and are of such a nature as to create a clear and present danger that they will bring about the substantive evils that Congress has a right to prevent. It is a question of proximity and degree."

This is a rule of reason. Correctly applied, it will preserve the right of free speech both from suppression by tyrannous, well-meaning majorities, and from abuse by irresponsible, fanatical minorities. Like many other rules for human conduct, it can be applied correctly only by the exercise of good judgment; and to the exercise of good judgment calmness is, in times of deep feeling and on subjects which excite passion, as essential as fearlessness and honesty.[92] The question whether in a particular instance the words spoken or written fall within the permissible curtailment of free speech is, under the rule enunciated by this Court, one of degree; and because it is a question of degree the field in which the jury may exercise its judgment is necessarily a wide one. But its field is not unlimited. The trial provided for is one by judge *and* jury, and the judge may not abdicate his function. If the words were of such a nature and were used under such circumstances that men, judging in calmness, could not reasonably say that they created a clear and present danger, that they would bring about the evil which Congress sought and had a right to prevent, then it is the duty of the trial judge to withdraw the case from the consideration of the jury; and, if he fails to do so, it is the duty of the appellate court to correct the error. . . .

The nature and possible effect of a writing cannot be properly determined by culling here and there a sentence and presenting it separated from the context. . . . Sometimes it is necessary to consider, in connection with it, other

---

[92] See Calmness.

evidence which may enlarge or otherwise control its meaning, or which may show that it was circulated under circumstances which gave it a peculiar significance or effect. . . .

The jury which found men guilty for publishing news items or editorials like those here in question must have supposed it to be within their province to condemn men, not merely for disloyal acts, but for a disloyal heart; provided only that the disloyal heart was evidenced by some utterance. To prosecute men for such publications reminds of the days when men were hanged for constructive treason. And, indeed, the jury may well have believed from the charge that the Espionage Act had in effect restored the crime of constructive treason. To hold that such harmless additions to or omissions from news items, and such impotent expressions of editorial opinion, as were here shown, can afford the basis even of a prosecution, will doubtless discourage criticism of the policies of the Government. To hold that such publications can be suppressed as false reports, subjects to new perils the constitutional liberty of the press, already seriously curtailed in practice under powers assumed to have been conferred upon the postal authorities. Nor will this grave danger end with the passing of the war. The constitutional right of free speech has been declared to be the same in peace and in war. In peace, too, men may differ widely as to what loyalty to our country demands; and an intolerant majority, swayed by passion or by fear, may be prone in the future, as it has often been in the past, to stamp as disloyal opinions with which it disagrees. Convictions such as these, besides abridging freedom of speech, threaten freedom of thought and of belief.

*

Full and free exercise of this right [to teach the truth as he sees it] by the citizen is ordinarily also his duty; for its exercise is more important to the Nation than it is to him-

self. Like the course of the heavenly bodies, harmony in
national life is a resultant of the struggle between contending forces.[93] In frank expression of conflicting opinion lies
the greatest promise of wisdom in governmental action; and
in suppression lies ordinarily the greatest peril.

*

The right to speak freely concerning functions of the Federal Government is a privilege of immunity of every citizen
of the United States which, even before the adoption of the
Fourteenth Amendment, a State was powerless to curtail.

*

[155] Although the rights of free speech and assembly are
fundamental, they are not in their nature absolute. Their
exercise is subject to restriction, if the particular restriction
proposed is required in order to protect the State from destruction or from serious injury, political, economic, or
moral. That the necessity which is essential to a valid restriction does not exist unless speech would produce, or is
intended to produce, a clear and imminent danger of some
substantive evil which the State constitutionally may seek
to prevent has been settled.

*

The powers of the courts to strike down an offending law
are no less when the interests involved are not property
rights, but the fundamental personal rights of free speech
and assembly.

*

I am unable to assent to the suggestion in the opinion of
the Court that assembling with a political party, formed to
advocate the desirability of a proletarian revolution by mass
action at some date necessarily far in the future, is not a
right within the protection of the Fourteenth Amendment.

---

[93] Repeated under Harmony in National Life.

*

The fundamental right of free men to strive for better conditions through new legislation and new institutions will not be preserved, if efforts to secure it by argument to fellow citizens may be construed as criminal incitement to disobey the existing law—merely because the argument presented seems to those exercising the judicial power to be unfair in its portrayal of existing evils, mistaken in its assumptions, unsound in reasoning, or intemperate in language. No objections more serious than these can, in my opinion, reasonably be made to the arguments presented in *The Price We Pay*.

FUNCTION OF SPEECH

It is the function of speech to free men from the bondage of irrational fears.[94]

GOD'S PRESENCE

[160] I do not understand what you mean by experiencing God's presence. I have faced many trials, had to make grave decisions, tasted of the sweet and bitter, was depressed and elated, worked and studied, and thought and meditated. I have lived through many a moment in which, according to the faithful, God should have spoken and helped. But I cannot say that he did or didn't. I sensed no power outside of myself working along with me. Nor would I describe what was going on in me as supernatural, irrational, or mysterious. I believe that I was reasoning through by concentrating and recalling what good men had said and done before me. To say that it was God who inspired me to give up my private practice and fight for women's welfare and against monopolies is to employ language that, I repeat, I do not understand. I have now and then come across plausible reasons for the existence of God but never what I should call proof.

---

[94] See Freedom of Speech.

And definitely never have I met a man who spoke convincingly of experiencing God's presence.

GOD'S PURPOSE

In cross-examining a witness I tried to establish the truth or falsity of what he was saying. I probed into his mind to know what was going on there. But I should not say that my efforts were altogether successful. There was always an area of doubt, barred cells, that remained sealed off. How then can I hope to read the Cosmic Mind, as you call it, or divine its purpose?

GOOD BARGAIN

The old idea of a good bargain was a transaction in which one man got the better of another. The new idea of a good contract is a transaction which is good for both parties to it.

GOVERNMENT AS LAWBREAKER

Decency, security, and liberty alike demand that Government officials shall be subjected to the same rules of conduct that are commands to the citizen. In a government of law, existence of the government will be imperiled if it fails to observe the law scrupulously. Our Government is the potent, the omnipresent teacher. For good or for ill, it teaches the whole people by its example. Crime is contagious. If the Government becomes a lawbreaker, it breeds contempt for law; it invites every man to become a law unto himself; it invites anarchy. To declare that in the administration of the criminal law the end justifies the means—to declare that the Government may commit crimes in order to secure the conviction of a private criminal—would bring terrible retribution. Against that pernicious doctrine this Court should resolutely set its face.

Justice Brandeis · 89

*

The Government may set decoys to entrap criminals. But it may not provoke or create a crime and then punish the criminal, its creature.

GOVERNMENT CONTROL

[165] I have no rigid social philosophy. I have been too intense on concrete problems of practical justice. And yet I can see that the tendency is steadily toward governmental control. The Government must keep order *not only physically but socially*. In old times the law was meant to protect each citizen from oppression by physical force. But we have passed to a subtler civilization; from oppression by force we have come to oppression in other ways. And the law must still protect a man from the things that rob him of his freedom, whether the oppressing force be physical or of a subtler kind.[95]

GOVERNMENT EMPLOYEES

We want men to think. We want every man in the service, of the three or four hundred thousand who are there, to recognize that he is a part of the governing body, and that on him rests responsibility within the limits of his employment just as much as upon the man on top. They cannot escape such responsibility. . . . They cannot be worthy of the respect and admiration of the people unless they add to the virtue of obedience some other virtues—the virtues of manliness, of truth, of courage, of willingness to risk positions, of the willingness to risk criticisms, of the willingness to risk the misunderstandings that so often come when people do the heroic thing.

GOVERNMENT INTRUSION

Experience should teach us to be most on our guard to protect liberty when the Government's purposes are benefi-

[95] See also Law and Life, Law's Function, Lawyers' Special Obligation.

cent. Men born to freedom are naturally alert to repel invasion of their liberty by evil-minded rulers. The greatest
dangers to liberty lurk in insidious encroachment by men
of zeal, well-meaning but without understanding.[96]

*

The makers of our Constitution undertook to secure conditions favorable to the pursuit of happiness. They recognized the significance of man's spiritual nature, of his feelings, and of his intellect. They knew that only a part of the
pain, pleasure, and satisfactions of life are to be found in
material things. They sought to protect Americans in their
beliefs, their thoughts, their emotions, and their sensations.
They conferred, as against the Government, the right to be
let alone—the most comprehensive of rights and the right
most valued by civilized men. To protect that right, every
unjustifiable intrusion by the Government upon the privacy
of the individual, whatever the means employed, must be
deemed a violation of the Fourth Amendment. And the use,
as evidence in a criminal proceeding, of facts ascertained by
such intrusion must be deemed a violation of the Fifth.[97]

GREATEST DANGER

There cannot be liberty without financial independence,
and the greatest danger to the people of the United States
today is in becoming, as they are gradually more and more,
a class of employees.[98]

GREATEST ECONOMIC MENACE

[170] The economic menace of past ages was the *dead
hand,* which gradually acquired a large part of all available
lands. The greatest economic menace of today is a very

---

[96] Repeated under Liberty's Greatest Danger; see also Wire Tapping.
[97] See also Wire Tapping.
[98] See also Financial Dependence, Financial Independence, Industrial Absolutism.

live hand, these great insurance companies which control so large a part of our quick capital.

GREATEST GOOD OF GREATEST NUMBER

Here and there you will find a hero—red-blooded, and courageous—loving manhood more than wealth, place or security—who dared to fight for independence and won. Here and there you may find the martyr, who resisted in silence and suffered with resignation. But America, which seeks "the greatest good of the greatest number," cannot be content with conditions that fit only the hero, the martyr or the slave.[99]

GREATEST MENACE TO FREEDOM

The greatest menace to freedom is an inert people.[1]

GREATEST PROBLEM

The Greatest Problem before the American people in this generation [is] the problem of reconciling our industrial system with the political democracy in which we live.

GREAT PHYSICIANS

The great physicians are those who in addition to that knowledge of therapeutics which is open to all, know not merely the human body but the human mind and emotions, so as to make themselves the proper diagnosis—to know the truth which their patients failed to disclose and who add to this an influence over the patient which is apt to spring from a real understanding of him.[2]

HALF FREE AND HALF SLAVE

[175] We are confronted in the twentieth century, as we were in the nineteenth century, with an irreconcilable con-

---

[99] See America, American Ideals.
[1] See Freedom of Speech.
[2] Repeated under Lawyers' Knowledge.

flict. Our democracy cannot endure half free and half slave. The essence of the trust is a combination of the capitalist, by the capitalist, for the capitalist.[3]

ALEXANDER HAMILTON

Hamilton was an apostle of the living law.

HARMONY IN NATIONAL LIFE

Like the course of the heavenly bodies, harmony in national life is a resultant of the struggle between contending forces.[4]

HEBREW LANGUAGE

Perhaps the most extraordinary achievement in Jewish nationalism is the revival of the Hebrew language, making it again a language for the common intercourse of men. The Hebrew Tongue, called a dead language for so many centuries, has, in the Jewish colonies and Jerusalem, become again a living Mother Tongue. The effect of this common language in unifying the Jews is of course great. For the Jews of Palestine came literally from the lands of the earth, each speaking, except for the use of Yiddish or Spaniolish, the language of the country from which he came, and each remaining almost a stranger to the others. But the effect of the Renaissance of the Hebrew Tongue is far greater than that of unifying the Jews. It is a potent factor in reviving the essentially Jewish spirit.

*

It was no ordinary sense of piety that made Ben Jehuda seek to introduce the Hebrew language. He recognized what the leaders of other peoples seeking rebirth and independence have recognized—that it is through the national language, expressing the peoples' soul, that the national spirit

---

[3] Repeated under Monopoly.
[4] See Freedom of Speech.

is aroused, and the national power restored. Despite the prevalence of the English Tongue in Ireland, the revival of Gaelic became one of the most important factors in the movement which has just resulted in securing for the Irish their long-coveted home rule. The revival of Flemish was a potent factor in the rebirth of the Belgian people, who are now giving such good account of themselves. And so it was with the revival of Greek, of Bulgarian, and of Serbian.

THEODOR HERZL

[180] Among Theodor Herzl's contributions to our understanding of the Jewish problem are these:

FIRST: The recognition of the fundamental fact that the Jews are a people—one people.

SECOND: The recognition of the political truth that the emancipation of the Jews can come only through themselves; that is, by democratic means.

HISTORY

History is not life. But since only life makes history the union of the two is obvious.

HOME LIFE

With the improvement in home life, the tone of the entire community is raised.[5]

HOW HUMAN BEINGS IMPROVE

Human beings . . . can be raised, and raised only, by holding up before them that which is higher and that which is better than they.

HUMAN NATURE

Human nature, like the inanimate, seeks the path of least resistance. To think hard and persistently is painful.[6]

---

[5] Repeated under Short Workday.
[6] Repeated under Thinking.

*

[185]   The weakness of human nature prevents men from being good judges of their own deservings.[7]

*

Human nature is such that monopolies, however well intentioned and however well regulated, inevitably become oppressive, arbitrary, unprogressive and inefficient.[8]

*

Human nature . . . is never wholly cast down by the misfortunes and frailties of our neighbors.[9]

HUMAN TRUTH

Labor must have throughout an opportunity of testing whether that which is recorded as a truth, is really a truth, and whether it is the whole truth. Labor must not only be convinced of the industrial truths—which scientific management is disclosing—but must be convinced that those truths are consistent with what may be termed human truth.[10]

IMMORTALITY OF THE SOUL[11]

I never read anything on the immortality of the soul, and I admit having read but little on the subject, that convinced me of its truth. What surprises me is that men should be longing for an afterlife in which there would apparently be nothing to do except to delight in heaven's wonders. For, as the theologians have pictured the afterlife, man will be there *sine* body and his soul will rejoin the Deity. If this is so then intellectual pursuits will come to an end with bodily exertions, for, as a part of the Deity, man will be in possession of all knowledge, leaving nothing to occupy him except

---

[7] See Bankers' Power.
[8] Repeated under Monopoly.
[9] See Blighting Influence of Journalistic Gossip.
[10] See also Labor's Share.
[11] See also Jews and Democracy.

some kind of spiritual enjoyment. But enjoyment, I thought, was more pagan than Jewish or Christian.

INDIFFERENCE

[190]   I do not consider indifference insuperable.

INDIVIDUALITY OF PEOPLES[12]

Deeply imbedded in every nation and people is the desire for full development—the longing for self-expression. In the past it has been generally assumed that the full development of one people necessarily involved its domination over others. Strong nations are apt to become convinced that by such domination only does civilization advance. Strong nations assume their own superiority, and come to believe that they possess the divine right to subject other peoples to their sway. Soon the belief in the existence of such a right becomes converted into a conviction that a duty exists to enforce it. Wars of aggrandizement follow as a natural result of this belief.

This attitude of nations and peoples is the exact correlative of the position generally assumed by the strong in respect to other individuals before democracy became a common possession. The struggles of the eighteenth and nineteenth centuries, both in peace and in war, were devoted largely to overcoming that position as to individuals, to establishing the equal right to development of every person, and in making clear that equal opportunity for all involves this necessary limitation: each man may develop himself so far, but only so far as his doing so will not interfere with the exercise of a like right by all others. Thus liberty has come to mean the right to enjoy life, to acquire property, to pursue happiness, in such manner that the exercise of the right in each is consistent with the exercise of a like

[12] See also Jewish Individuality, Liberalism and Anti-Jewish Prejudice, National Individuality.

right by every other of our fellow citizens. Liberty thus defined underlies twentieth-century democracy. Liberty thus defined exists in a large part of the western world. And even where this equal right of all has not yet been accepted as a political right, its ethical value is becoming recognized.[13]

The movements of the last century have proved that whole peoples have individuality no less marked than that of the single person; that the individuality of a people is irrepressible, and that internationalism which seeks the obliteration of nations or peoples is unattainable.[14] As democracy rejects the proposal of the superman who shall rise through sacrifice of the many and insists that the full development of each individual is not only a right but a duty to society; so the new nationalism proclaims the right and the duty of each race or people to develop itself fully. . . .

No peace which is lasting can ever come until the nations, great and small, accept the democratic principle that there is and shall be no supernation, to rise through subjection of others, and the truth that each people has in it something of peculiar value which it can contribute to that civilization for which we are all striving. And until that principle is accepted, and that truth recognized, unrest must be unending. Whatever economic arrangement may be made, however perfect and comprehensive may become the machinery for enforcing the treaties of the nations, those peoples who are not accorded equality of opportunity for full development will prove a source of irritation; injustice will bring its inevitable penalty; and the peace of the world will be broken again and again, as those little nations of the Balkans have taught us in recent years.

Equal opportunity for all people as for all individuals—that is the essential of international as well as of national justice upon which a peace which is to be permanent must

---

[13] Repeated under Liberty.
[14] Repeated under National Individuality.

rest. Unless that fundamental right is recognized and granted universally, there will be discord and war in the future, as there has been in the past.

INDIVIDUAL SUFFERING

We cannot cope with individual suffering unless we succeed in removing the cause of that suffering.

INDUSTRIAL ABSOLUTISM [15]

The next generation must witness a continuing and ever-increasing contest between those who have and those who have not. The industrial world is in a state of ferment. The ferment is in the main peaceful, and, to a considerable extent, silent; but there is felt today very widely the inconsistency in this condition of political democracy and industrial absolutism. The people are beginning to doubt whether in the long run democracy and absolutism can coexist in the same community; beginning to doubt whether there is a justification for the great inequalities in the distribution of wealth, for the rapid creation of fortunes, more mysterious than the deeds of Aladdin's lamp. The people have begun to think; and they show evidences on all sides of a tendency to act.[16]

INDUSTRIAL DEMOCRACY

Unrest, to my mind, never can be removed—and fortunately never can be removed—by mere improvement of the physical and material condition of the workingman. If it were possible we should run great risk of improving their material condition and reducing their manhood. We must bear in mind all the time that however much we may desire material improvement and must desire it for the comfort of the individual, that the United States is a democracy, and that we must have, above all things, men. It is the develop-

---

[15] See also Financial Dependence.
[16] See also Monopoly.

ment of manhood to which any industrial and social system should be directed. We Americans are committed not only to social justice in the sense of avoiding things which bring suffering and harm, like unjust distribution of wealth; but we are committed primarily to democracy. The social justice for which we are striving is an incident of our democracy, not the main end. It is rather the result of democracy—perhaps its finest expression—but it rests upon democracy, which implies the rule by the people.[17] And therefore the end for which we must strive is the attainment of rule by the people, and that involves industrial democracy as well as political democracy. That means that the problems of a trade should no longer be the problems of the employer alone. The problems of his business, and it is not the employer's business alone, are the problems of all in it. The union cannot shift upon the employer the responsibility for conditions, nor can the employer insist upon determining, according to his will the conditions which shall exist. The problems which exist are the problems of the trade; they are the problems of employer and employee. Profit sharing, however liberal, cannot meet the situation. That would merely mean dividing the profits of business. Such a division may do harm or it might do good, dependent on how it is applied.

There must be a division not only of profits, but a division also of responsibilities. The employees must have the opportunity of participating in the decisions as to what shall be their condition and how the business shall be run. They must learn also in sharing that responsibility that they must bear, too, the suffering arising from grave mistakes, just as the employer must. But the right to assist in making the decisions, the right of making their own mistakes, if mistakes there must be, is a privilege which should not be de-

---

[17] See American Ideals.

nied to labor. We must insist upon labor sharing the responsibility for the result of the business.[18]

*

[195]   Prolonged peace and prosperity can rest only on the foundation of industrial liberty. Industrial democracy should ultimately attend political democracy. Industrial absolutism is not merely impossible in this country at the present time, but is most undesirable. Our employers can no more afford to be absolute masters of their employees than they can afford to submit to the mastery of their employees.[19]

*

Liberty is the greatest developer. Herodotus tells us that while the tyrants ruled, the Athenians were no better fighters than their neighbors; but when freed, they immediately surpassed all others.[20] If industrial democracy—true cooperation—should be substituted for industrial absolutism, there would be no lack of industrial leaders.

*

All of our human experience shows that no one with absolute power can be trusted to give it up even in part. That has been the experience with political absolutism; it must prove the same with industrial absolutism. Industrial democracy will not come by gift. It has got to be won by those who desire it.

INDUSTRIAL DEMOCRACY AND THINKING

One hundred years ago the civilized world did not believe that it was possible that the people could rule themselves; they did not believe that it was possible to have government of the people, by the people, and for the people. America in the last century proved that democracy is a success.[21]

---

[18] See also Unrest.
[19] See Employer and Employee.
[20] Repeated under Liberty.
[21] See America.

The civilized world today believes that in the industrial world self-government is impossible; that we must adhere to the system which we have known as the monarchical system, the system of master and servant, or, as now more politely called, employer and employee. It rests with this century and perhaps with America to prove that as we have in the political world shown what self-government can do, we are to pursue the same lines in the industrial world.

And what will that involve? I take it: free thinking. In the first place, of course, whether we have an institution mastered by the employer and employee in the old form or in the form of industrial democracy to which we look forward, we shall have Obedience. But the obedience will be this: it will be obedience to the laws which the people make for themselves in a business, and not the laws which are made for them and in the making of which they have no part. That is the first difference between this industrial democracy to which we look forward and the old monarchical form.

In the next place, we have a condition in which these laws are made for the benefit or mainly for the benefit of those who make them, and that is, who do the work.

And in the third place, we have leaders of industry instead of masters of industry or captains of industry.

Those are the great differences.

And how are they to be attained?

I take it, also, that there are three things essential. In the first place, those who engage in the effort of freeing industry, or becoming free, must note this: that in order not to have someone as master, they must be master of themselves. That is the first rule.

The second rule is: that when they work, they must work with and for others, for the institution of which they are a part.

The third rule is that they must think. Democracy is only

possible, industrial democracy, among people who think; among people who are above the average intelligence. And that thinking is not a heaven-born thing, that intelligence is not a gift that merely comes. It is a gift men make and women make for themselves. It is earned, and it is earned by effort. There is no effort, to my mind, that is comparable in its qualities, that is so taxing to the individual, as to think, to analyze fundamentally.[22]

The brain is like the hand. It grows with using.[23]

INDUSTRIAL INJUSTICE

The real fight today is against the inhuman, relentless exercise of capitalistic power. First we had the struggle for independence, and the second great struggle in our history was to keep the nation whole and abolish slavery. The present struggle in which we are engaged is for social and industrial justice.

INDUSTRIAL LIBERTY[24]

[200] Prolonged peace and prosperity can rest only upon the foundation of industrial liberty. The peace which employers should seek is not the peace of fifty years ago, when the employers were absolute masters of the situation. The peace which the employers should seek is not the peace of mediaeval guilds, with their numberless restrictions. Industrial liberty must attend political liberty. The lead which America takes in the industrial world is no doubt due to our unbounded resources; but of these resources none are so great as the spirit and the ability incident to a free people. We lead the world industrially, not so much because the resources of nature are unbounded, as because the faculties and aspirations of men are comparatively unfettered.

---

[22] Repeated under Thinking.
[23] See Brain.
[24] See also Financial Dependence.

*

"Man cannot live by bread alone." Men must have industrial liberty as well as good wages.

*

Can this contradiction—our grand political liberty and this industrial slavery—long coexist? Either political liberty will be extinguished or industrial liberty must be restored.

*

You cannot have true American citizenship, you cannot preserve political liberty, you cannot secure American standards of living unless some degree of industrial liberty accompanies it.

*

Industrial liberty must rest upon reasonableness. We gain nothing by exchanging the tyranny of capital for the tyranny of labor. Arbitrary demands must be met by determined refusals, also at any cost.

*

[205] Industrial liberty, like civil liberty, must rest upon the solid foundation of law. Disregard the law in either, however good your motives, and you have anarchy.

*

Both liberty and democracy are seriously threatened by the growth of big business. Today the need is not so much for freedom from physical restraint as for freedom from economic oppression.

Already the displacement of the small independent business man by the huge corporation with its myriad of employees, its absentee ownership, and its financier control, presents a grave danger to our democracy. The social loss is great; and there is no economic gain.

Political liberty, then, is not enough; it must be attended by economic and industrial liberty.[25]

INTELLIGENT SELF-INTEREST

To reduce the price of gas we need not only honesty but also skill, energy and initiative. And this may be best secured by following those lines of intelligent self-interest upon which the remarkable industrial advance of America has proceeded.

INTERLOCKING DIRECTORATES[26]

There is another reason why interlocking directorates must be abolished: namely, the demands of efficiency. Obviously the only justification for the director's existence is that he should direct; which means that he should be an absolutely fair and intelligent adviser and critic of the enterprise. The men who are in charge of an enterprise as executive officers are supposed to manage, and to possess the required energy and determination to go forward. But in a well-equipped organization there should be men who will check up the manager's judgment and performance. Only in this way can continued prosperity be assured.

For the proper exercise of the functions of director, it is essential that he be disinterested; that is, be free from any conflicting interest. But it is also essential that he have knowledge. Facts, facts, facts, are the only basis on which he can properly exercise his judgment. It is as necessary that he know intimately the facts concerning the business, as that he have only one interest to subserve. Now, no man can have such detailed knowledge of the facts of many enterprises. This is due to the limitations of time and place and to those other limits set by nature upon human intelligence. How can one man know in respect to many large corpora-

---

[25] See also Liberty, Big Business, Monopoly.
[26] See also Monopoly.

tions the facts which a director needs to know in order to insure efficient management? [27]

*

My objection to interlocking directorates is not on the assumption that men mean to do wrong. It is because it is humanly impossible for a man representing conflicting interests on two boards to do right by both, no matter how pure his purpose is.

*

[210]   The practice of interlocking directorates is the root of many evils. It offends laws human and divine. Applied to rival corporations, it tends to the suppression of competition and to violation of the Sherman Law. Applied to corporations which deal with each other, it tends to disloyalty and to violation of the fundamental law that no man can serve two masters. In either event it tends to inefficiency; for it removes incentive and destroys soundness of judgment. It is undemocratic, for it rejects the platform: "A fair field and no favors"—substituting the pull of privilege for the push of manhood. It is the most potent instrument of the Money Trust. Break the control so exercised by the investment bankers over railroads, public-service and industrial corporations, over banks, life insurance and trust companies, and a long step will have been taken toward attainment of the New Freedom.[28]

INVESTOR'S SERVILITY

The large army of small investors, constituting a substantial majority of all security buyers, are entirely free from banker control. Their submission is undoubtedly due, in part, to the fact that the bankers control the avenues to recognizedly safe investments almost as fully as they do the

---

[27] See also Efficiency.
[28] See also Bankers' Power. Repeated under New Freedom.

avenues to capital. But the investor's servility is due partly, also, to his ignorance of the facts. Is it not probable that, if each investor knew the extent to which the security he buys from the banker is diluted by excessive underwritings, commissions and profits, there would be a strike of capital against these unjust exactions?

IRREGULARITY OF EMPLOYMENT

Irregularity of employment creates hardships and demoralization of every kind. It is the most sinful waste.[29]

*

Irregularity in employment—the greatest of our evils—cannot be overcome unless production and consumption are more nearly balanced.[30]

JEW—DEFINITION OF TERM

Councils of rabbis and others have undertaken at times to prescribe by definition that only those shall be deemed Jews who professedly adhere to the orthodox or reformed faith. But in the connection in which we are considering the term, it is certainly not in the power of any single body of Jews, or indeed of all Jews collectively, to establish the effective definition. The meaning of the word Jewish in the term Jewish Problem must be accepted as coextensive with the disabilities which it is our problem to remove. It is the non-Jews who create the disabilities and in so doing give definition to the term Jew. Those disabilities extend substantially to all of Jewish blood. The disabilities do not end with a renunciation of faith, however sincere. They do not end with the elimination, however complete, of external Jewish mannerisms. The disabilities do not end ordinarily until the Jewish blood has been so thoroughly diluted by repeated

---

[29] Repeated under Sinful Waste.
[30] See Experimentation.

inter-marriages as to result in practically obliterating the Jew.

And we Jews, by our own acts, give a like definition to the term Jew. When men and women of Jewish blood suffer, because of that fact, and even if they suffer from quite different causes, our sympathy and our help goes out to them instinctively in whatever country they may live and without inquiring into the shades of their belief or unbelief. When those of Jewish blood exhibit moral or intellectual superiority, genius or special talent, we feel pride in them, even if they have abjured the faith like Spinoza, Marx, Disraeli or Heine. Despite the meditations of pundits or the decrees of council, our own instincts and acts, and those of others, have defined for us the term Jew.

JEWISH ATTRIBUTES

[215]   To take risks is the very essence of Jewish life, that is, to take necessary risks. The wise man seeks not to avoid but to minimize risks. He minimizes them by using judgment and by knowledge and by thinking. These are, fortunately, preeminently Jewish attributes.

JEWISH FESTIVALS

I do not believe that the manner in which some Jewish festivals are observed does full justice to the historic moments they celebrate or to the values they symbolize. When aging forms do hurt to content it is time to think of new form. A symbol should be transparent and not opaque and should speak eloquently and convincingly of the idea it represents.

JEWISH HERITAGE

It is not wealth, it is not station, it is not social standing and ambition which can make us worthy of the Jewish name, of the Jewish heritage. To be worthy of them, we must live up to and with them. We must regard ourselves as their custodians. Every young man here must feel that he is the trustee of what is best in Jewish history.[31]

JEWISH INDIVIDUALITY

We recognize that with each child the aim of education should be to develop his own individuality, not to make him an imitator, not to assimilate him to others. Shall we fail to recognize this truth when applied to whole peoples? And what people in the world has shown greater individuality than the Jews? Has any a nobler past? Does any possess common ideas better worth expressing? Has any marked traits worthier of development? Of all the peoples in the world those of two tiny states stand preeminent as contributors to our present civilization, the Greeks and the Jews. The Jews gave to the world its three greatest religions, reverence for law, and the highest conceptions of morality. Never before has the value of our contribution been so generally recognized. Our teaching of brotherhood and righteousness has, under the name of democracy and social justice, become the twentieth century striving of America and of western Europe. Our conception of law is embodied in the American constitution which proclaims this to be a "government of laws and not of men." And for the triumph of our other great teaching, the doctrine of peace, this cruel war is paving the way.[32]

JEWISH INTELLECTUAL CAPACITY

Our intellectual capacity was developed by the almost continuous training of the mind throughout twenty-five centuries. The Torah led the "People of the Book" to intellectual pursuits at times when most of the Aryan peoples were illiterate. Religion imposed the use of the mind upon the Jews, indirectly as well as directly. It demanded of the Jew

---

[31] Repeated under Trustee of History.
[32] See also Individuality of Peoples, Nationality.

not merely the love, but also the understanding of God. This necessarily involved a study of the Law. The conditions under which the Jews were compelled to live during the last two thousand years promoted study in a people among whom there was already considerable intellectual attainment. Throughout the centuries of persecution practically the only life open to the Jew which could give satisfaction was the intellectual and spiritual life. Other fields of activity and of distinction which divert men from intellectual pursuits were closed to Jews. Thus they were protected by their privations from the temptations of material things and worldly ambitions. Driven by circumstances to intellectual pursuits their mental capacity gradually developed. And as men delight in that which they do well, there was an ever-widening appreciation of things intellectual.

JEWISH "PECULIARITIES"

[220] Common race is only one of the elements which determine nationality. Conscious community of sentiments, common experiences, common qualities are equally, perhaps more, important. Religion, traditions and customs bound us together, though scattered throughout the world. The similarity of experience tended to produce similarity of qualities and community of sentiments. Common suffering so intensified the feeling of brotherhood as to overcome largely all the influences making for diversification. The segregation of the Jew was so general, so complete, and so long continued as to intensify our "peculiarities" and make them almost ineradicable.

JEWISH PEOPLE—ITS PRESERVATION

Throughout long years which represent my own life, I have been to a great extent separated from Jews. I am very ignorant in things Jewish. But recent experiences, public and professional, have taught me this: I find Jews possessed of those very qualities which we of the twentieth century seek to develop in our struggle for justice and democracy; a deep moral feeling which makes them capable of noble acts; a deep sense of the brotherhood of man; and a high intelligence, the fruit of three thousand years of civilization.

These experiences have made me feel that the Jewish people have something which should be saved for the world; that the Jewish people should be preserved; and that it is our duty to pursue that method of saving which most promises success.

JEWISH PERSECUTION

The suffering of the Jews due to injustices continuing throughout nearly twenty centuries is the greatest tragedy in history. Never was the aggregate of such suffering larger than today. Never were the injustices more glaring.

*

I suppose eighteen centuries of Jewish persecution must have enured me to such hardships and developed the like of a duck's back.

JEWISH PROBLEM

For us the Jewish Problem means this: How can we secure for Jews, wherever they may live, the same rights and opportunities enjoyed by non-Jews? How can we secure for the world the full contribution which Jews can make, if unhampered by artificial limitations?

The problem has two aspects: That of the individual Jew, and that of Jews collectively. Obviously, no individual should be subjected anywhere, by reason of the fact that he is a Jew, to a denial of any common right or opportunity enjoyed by non-Jews. But Jews collectively should likewise enjoy the same right and opportunity to live and develop as do other groups of people. This right of development on the part of the group is essential to the full enjoyment of rights by the individual. For the individual is dependent for his development (and his happiness) in large part upon the development of the group of which he forms a part. We can scarcely conceive of an individual German or Frenchman living and developing without some relation to the contemporary German or French life and culture. And since death is not a solution of the problem of life, the solution of the Jewish Problem necessarily involves the continued existence of the Jews as Jews.

JEWISH SPIRIT AND AMERICA

[225] There is no inconsistency between loyalty to America and loyalty to Jewry. The Jewish spirit, the product of our religion and experiences, is essentially modern and essentially American. Not since the destruction of the Temple have the Jews in spirit and in ideals been so fully in harmony with the noblest aspirations of the country in which they lived.

America's fundamental law seeks to make real the brotherhood of man.[33] That brotherhood became the Jewish fundamental law more than twenty-five hundred years ago. America's insistent demand in the twentieth century is for social justice.[34] That also has been the Jews' striving for ages. Their affliction as well as their religion has prepared the Jews for effective democracy. Persecution broadened their sympathies. It trained them in patient endurance, in self-control, and in sacrifice. It made them think as well as suffer. It deepened the passion for righteousness.

JEWISH SURVIVAL

We have survived persecution because of the virtues and sacrifices of our ancestors.

---

[33] See America's Fundamental Law.
[34] See America's Insistent Demand.

JEWS AND DEMOCRACY

Among the Jews democracy was not an ideal merely. It was a practice, a practice made possible by the existence among them of certain conditions essential to successful democracy, namely:

First: An all-pervading sense of duty in the citizen. Democratic ideals cannot be attained through emphasis merely upon the rights of man. Even a recognition that every right has a correlative duty will not meet the needs of democracy. Duty must be accepted as the dominant conception in life.[35] Such were the conditions in the early days of the colonies and states of New England, when American democracy reached there its fullest expression; for the Puritans were trained in implicit obedience to stern duty by constant study of the Prophets.[36]

Second: Relatively high intellectual attainments. Democratic ideals cannot be attained by the mentally undeveloped. In a government where everyone is part sovereign, everyone should be competent, if not to govern, at least to understand the problems of government; and to this end education is an essential.[37] The early New Englanders appreciated fully that education is an essential of potential equality. The founding of their common school system was coincident with founding of the colonies; and even the establishment of institutions for higher education did not lag far behind. Harvard College was founded but six years after the first settlement of Boston.[38]

Third: Submission to leadership as distinguished from authority. Democratic ideals can be attained only where those who govern exercise their power not by alleged divine right or inheritance, but by force of character and intelli-

---

[35] See Duty.
[36] Repeated under Puritans.
[37] See Democratic Ideals.
[38] See Early New Englanders.

gence.[39] Such a condition implies the attainment by citizens generally of relatively high moral and intellectual standards; and such a condition actually existed among the Jews. These men who were habitually denied rights, and whose province it has been for centuries "to suffer and to think," learned not only to sympathize with their fellows (which is the essence of a democracy and social justice), but also to accept voluntarily the leadership of those highly endowed, morally and intellectually.

Fourth: A developed community sense. The sense of duty to which I have referred was particularly effective in promoting democratic ideals among the Jews, because of their deep-seated community feeling. To describe the Jew as an individualist is to state a most misleading half-truth. He has to a rare degree merged his individuality and his interests in the community of which he forms a part. This is evidenced among other things by his attitude toward immortality. Nearly every other people has reconciled this world of suffering with the idea of a beneficent Providence by conceiving of immortality for the individual. The individual sufferer bore present ills by regarding this world as merely the preparation for another, in which those living righteously here would find individual reward hereafter. Of all nations, Israel "takes precedence in suffering"; but, despite our national tragedy, the doctrine of individual immortality found relatively slight lodgment among us.[40]

JEWS TODAY

I believe that the Jews can be just as much of a priest people today as they ever were in the prophetic days.[41]

---

[39] See Democratic Ideals, Character and Intelligence.
[40] See also Immortality of the Soul.
[41] See also Chosen People.

JOINERS[42]

Multiplicity of pursuits is as great a curse as bigness. The greatest benefactors of the human race have not been they who attempted many things but they who did a few things well. The growing propensity of Americans to "join" is bound to result in indifference to all organizations and in organizational bureaucracies.

JOSEPH

[230]   Our ancestor Joseph who realized that there were lean years as well as fat ones knew a thing or two.

JUDGES

I believe that our judges are as honest as you can make men. But like all the rest of us they are subject to their environment and law has always been a narrowing, conservatizing profession.[43] In England it was always easy for a Tory government to find great lawyers for judicial office but for a liberal government it was hard. And so it has been throughout history. Nearly all of England's great lawyers were Tories.

*

The judge came to the bench unequipped with the necessary knowledge of economic and social science, and his judgments suffered likewise through lack of equipment in the lawyers who presented the cases to him. For a judge rarely performs his functions adequately unless the case before him is adequately presented. Thus were the blind led by the blind. It is not surprising that under such conditions the laws as administered failed to meet contemporary economic and social demands.[44]

---

[42] See also Monopoly.
[43] Repeated under Law and Life.
[44] Repeated under Lawyers' Education.

*

What we must do in America is not to attack our judges, but to educate them. All judges should be made to feel, as many judges already do, that the things needed to protect liberty are radically different from what they were fifty years back. In some courts the judges' conceptions of their own powers must also change. Some judges have decided a law unconstitutional simply because they considered the law unwise. These judges should be made to feel that they have no such right, that their business is not to decide whether the view taken by the legislature is a wise view, but whether a body of men could reasonably hold such a view. In the past the courts have reached their conclusions largely deductively from preconceived notions and precedents. The method I have tried to employ in arguing cases before them has been inductive, reasoning from the facts.[45]

JUSTICE

Justice can be attained only by a careful regard for fundamental facts, since justice is but truth in action.

LABOR'S SHARE[46]

[235] We ought to make up for the opportunity we lost when we changed from hand labor to machine labor. I think it is perfectly clear that when that change was made the employer got more than he ought to have got; and labor did not get its share, because labor was not organized. Now, when labor is to a very considerable extent organized, labor ought to insist upon scientific management. It has a just cause of complaint if a business is not well managed. Then, when the proceeds of good management are secured, labor ought to insist upon getting its share; and, as I have said, I think its share ought to be large, because of the reason that

[45] See Facts.
[46] See also Human Truth, Responsibility, Scientific Management.

when machines were introduced labor did not get its share.

LAW AND LIFE[47]

The law has everywhere a tendency to lag behind the facts of life.

*

Law has always been a narrowing, conservatizing profes.-sion.[48]

*

Modification implies growth. It is the life of the law.

LAW AND PUBLIC OPINION

Whether a law enacted in the exercise of the police power is just, subject to the charge of being unreasonable or arbitrary can ordinarily be determined only by a consideration of the contemporary conditions, social, industrial, and political, of the community to be affected thereby. Resort to such facts is necessary, among other things, in order to appreciate the evils sought to be remedied and the possible effects of the remedy proposed. Nearly all legislation involves a weighing of public needs as against private desires, and likewise a weighing of relative social values. Since government is not an exact science, prevailing public opinion concerning the evils and the remedy is among the important facts deserving consideration, particularly when the public conviction is both deep-seated and widespread and has been reached after deliberation.

LAW AND THE WILL OF THE PEOPLE

[240] Your former townsman, Charles R. Crane, told me once the story of two men whose lives he would have cared most to have lived. One was Bogigish, a native of the ancient

---

[47] See also Government Control, Living Law.
[48] See Judges.

city of Ragusa off the coast of Dalmatia—a deep student of
law, who after gaining some distinction at the University
of Vienna and in France, became Professor at the University of Odessa. When Montenegro was admitted to the
family of nations, its Prince concluded that, like other civilized countries, it must have a code of law. Bogigish's fame
had reached Montenegro, for Ragusa is but a few miles
distant. So the Prince begged the Czar of Russia to have
the learned jurist prepare a code for Montenegro. The Czar
granted the request, and Bogigish undertook the task. But
instead of utilizing his great knowledge of laws to draft a
code, he proceeded to Montenegro, and for two years literally made his home with the people,—studying everywhere
their customs, their practices, their needs, their beliefs, their
points of view. Then he embodied in law the life which the
Montenegrins lived. They respected that law, because it expressed the will of the people.

*

No law can be effective which does not take into consideration the conditions of the community for which it is
designed; no law can be a good law—every law must be a
bad law—that remains unenforced.

LAW'S FUNCTION[49]

No small part of the law's function is to make men good.

LAWS NOT MEN[50]

The way to correct the evil of an unjust decision is not
to evade the law but to amend it. The unions should take
the position squarely that they are amenable to law, prepared to take the consequences if they transgress, and thus
show that they are in full sympathy with the spirit of our

[49] See also Government Control.
[50] See also Unions.

people, whose political system rests upon the proposition
that this is a government of law, and not of men.

*

Checks and balances were established in order that this
should be "a government of laws and not of men."

LAWYERS' EDUCATION

[245] The pursuit of the legal profession involves a happy
combination of the intellectual with the practical life. The
intellectual tends to breadth of view; the practical to that
realization of limitations which are essential to the wise conduct of life. Formerly the lawyer secured breadth of view
largely through wide professional experience. Being a general practitioner, he was brought into contact with all phases
of contemporary life. His education was not legal only,
because his diversified clientage brought him, by the mere
practice of his profession, an economic and social education.
The relative smallness of the communities tended to make
his practice diversified not only in the character of matters
dealt with, but also in the character or standing of his
clients. For the same lawyer was apt to serve at one time or
another both rich and poor, both employer and employee.
Furthermore, nearly every lawyer of ability took some part
in political life. Our greatest judges, Marshall, Kent, Story,
Shaw, had secured this training. . . .

The last fifty years have brought a great change in professional life. Industrial development and the consequent
growth of cities have led to a high degree of specialization
—specialization not only in the nature and class of questions
dealt with, but also specialization in the character of clientage. The term "corporation lawyer" is significant in this
connection.[51] The growing intensity of professional life
tended also to discourage participation in public affairs, and

---

[51] See also Corporation Lawyer.

thus the broadening of view which comes from political life
was lost. . . .

The effect of this contraction of the lawyers' intimate relation to contemporary life was doubly serious, because it
came at a time when the rapidity of our economic and
social transformation made accurate and broad knowledge
of present-day problems essential to the administration of
justice.

The judge came to the bench unequipped with the necessary knowledge of economic and social science, and his judgment suffered likewise through lack of equipment in the
lawyers who presented the cases to him. For a judge rarely
performs his functions adequately unless the case before him
is adequately presented. Thus were the blind led by the
blind. It is not surprising that under such conditions the
laws as administered failed to meet contemporary economic
and social demands. . . .[52]

We are powerless to restore the general practitioner and
general participation in public life. Intense specialization
must continue. But we can correct its distorting effects by
broader education—by study undertaken preparatory to
practice—and continued by lawyer and judge throughout
life; study of economics and sociology and politics which
embody the facts and present the problems of today.

LAWYERS' KNOWLEDGE

Knowledge of decisions and powers of logic are mere
handmaidens—they are servants, not masters. The control-
ling force is the deep knowledge of human necessities. It
was this which made Jessel the great lawyer and the greater
judge. The man who does not know intimately human
affairs is apt to make of the law a bed of Procrustes. No
hermit can be a great lawyer, least of all a commercial
lawyer. When from a knowledge of the law, you pass to its

---

[52] See Judges.

application, the need of a full knowledge of men and of their affairs becomes even more apparent. The duty of a lawyer today is not that of a solver of legal conundrums; he is indeed a counsellor of law. Knowledge of the law is of course essential to his efficiency, but the law bears to his profession a relation very similar to that which medicine does to that of the physicians. The apothecary can prepare the dose, the more intelligent one even knows the specific for most common diseases. It requires but a mediocre physician to administer the proper drug for the patient who correctly and fully describes his ailment. The great physicians are those who in addition to that knowledge of therapeutics which is open to all, know not merely the human body but the human mind and emotions, so as to make themselves the proper diagnosis—to know the truth which their patients fail to disclose and who add to this an influence over the patient which is apt to spring from a real understanding of him.[53]

LAWYERS' OPPORTUNITY

It is true that at the present time the lawyer does not hold that position with the people which he held fifty years ago; but the reason is in my opinion not lack of opportunity. It is because, instead of holding a position of independence between the wealthy and the people, prepared to curb the excesses of either, the able lawyers have to a great extent allowed themselves to become an adjunct of the great corporations, and have neglected their obligation to use their powers for the protection of the people. If we are to solve the important economic, social and industrial questions which have become political questions also, it seems to me clear that the attitude of the lawyer in this respect must be materially changed. . . . The great opportunity of the

[53] See Great Physicians.

American Bar is and will be to stand again as it did in the past, ready to protect also the interest of the people.

*

The people are beginning to doubt whether in the long run democracy and absolutism can coexist in the same community; beginning to doubt whether there is really a justification for the great inequalities in the distribution of wealth. This movement must necessarily progress; the people's thought will take shape in action. And it lies with our lawyers to say in what lines that action shall be expressed: wisely and temperately or wildly and intemperately; in lines of evolution or in lines of revolution.

LAWYERS' SPECIAL OBLIGATION [54]

We who are lawyers have a special obligation, and that is to make our law efficient. The disgrace that has come to the law, the discredit, the disrespect which has come to the law, is because it is inefficient, and because we make rules and we do not provide any machinery for enforcing them.

LAWYERS' TRAINING [55]

[250] The whole training of the lawyer leads to the development of judgment. His early training—his work with books in the study of legal rules—teaches him patient research and develops both the memory and the reasoning faculties. He becomes practiced in logic; and yet the use of the reasoning faculties in the study of law is very different from their use, say, in metaphysics. The lawyer's processes of reasoning, his logical conclusions, are being constantly tested by experience. He is running up against facts at every point. Indeed it is a maxim of the law: Out of the facts

[54] See also Government Control.
[55] See also Facts.

grows the law; that is, propositions are not considered abstractly, but always with reference to facts.

LEGAL PROFESSION [56]

Young men who feel drawn to the legal profession may rest assured that they will find in it an opportunity for usefulness which is probably unequalled elsewhere. There is and there will be a call upon the legal profession to do a great work for this country.

*

Our country is, after all, not a country of dollars, but of ballots. The immense corporate wealth will necessarily develop a hostility from which much trouble will come to us unless the excesses of capital are curbed, through the respect for law, as the excesses of democracy were curbed seventy-five years ago.[57] There will come a revolt of the people against the capitalists, unless the aspirations of the people are given some adequate legal expression; and to this end cooperation of the abler lawyers is essential.

LEGAL SCIENCE—DEAF AND BLIND

Political as well as economic and social science noted these revolutionary changes. But legal science—the unwritten or judge-made laws as distinguished from legislation —was largely deaf and blind to them. Courts continued to ignore newly arisen social needs. They applied complacently eighteenth century conceptions of the liberty of the individual and of the sacredness of private property. Early nineteenth century scientific half-truths, like "The survival of the fittest," which translated into practice meant "The devil take the hindmost," were erected by judicial sanction into a moral law.

---

[56] See also Corporation Lawyer.
[57] See Excesses of Capital.

LEISURE [58]

No people ever did or ever can attain a worthy civilization by the satisfaction merely of material needs, however high these needs are raised. The American standard of living demands not only a high minimum wage, but a high minimum of leisure, because we must meet also needs other than material ones.

*

[255] Serfdom, slavery, peonage, sweatshops held back progress for centuries. By bread alone or labor alone man can barely exist. To live and make life worth living he must have leisure to enjoy the fruits of his labor.

*

Leisure does not imply idleness. It means ability to work not less but more, ability to work at something besides breadwinning, ability to work harder while working at breadwinning, and ability to work more years at breadwinning. Leisure, so defined, is an essential of successful democracy.

*

The art of using leisure time, like any other, must be learned; but it is certain that the proper use of leisure, as of liberty, can never be attained except by those who have the opportunity of leisure or of liberty.

*

We need leisure, among other reasons, because with us every man is of the ruling class. Our education and condition of life must be such as become a ruler. Our great beneficent experiment in democracy will fail unless the people, our rulers, are developed in character and intelligence. [59]

---

[58] See also Short Workday.
[59] See Democratic Ideals.

LIBERALISM AND ANTI-JEWISH PREJUDICE

Why is it that liberalism has failed to eliminate the anti-Jewish prejudice? It is because the liberal movement has not yet brought full liberty. Enlightened countries grant to the individual equality before the law; but they fail still to recognize the equality of whole peoples or nationalities. We seek to protect as individuals those constituting a minority; but we fail to realize that protection cannot be complete unless group equality also is recognized.[60]

LIBERATION OF SMALLER PEOPLES

[260] The liberation of lesser nationalities is prominent among the hopeful results of the War. And yet their independence was won less by arms than the slow process of education. It was largely the work of far-seeing, patient, persistent devoted men and women, who awakened in the rising generation an interest in the language, the literature, the traditions of their people, and through the acquisition of knowledge, developed the striving for liberty and opportunity and the fuller life.

LIBERTY [61]

The history of Anglo-Saxon and of American liberty rests upon that struggle to resist wrong—to resist it at any cost when first offered rather than to pay the penalty of ignominious surrender.

*

The liberty of each individual must be limited in such a way that it leaves to others the possibility of individual liberty; the right to develop must be subject to that limitation which gives everybody else the right to develop; the restriction is merely an adjustment of the relations of one individual to another.

---

[60] See also Individuality of Peoples.
[61] See also Industrial Liberty.

*

I cannot believe that the liberty guaranteed by the Fourteenth Amendment includes only liberty to acquire and to enjoy property.

*

Liberty means exercising one's rights consistently with a like exercise of rights by other people; . . . liberty is distinguished from license in that it is subject to certain restrictions and that no one can expect to secure liberty in the sense in which we recognize it in America without having his rights curtailed in those respects in which it is necessary to limit them in the general public interest.[62]

*

[265]   Liberty has come to mean the right to enjoy life, to acquire property, to pursue happiness, in such manner that the exercise of the right in each is consistent with the exercise of a like right by every other of our fellow citizens. Liberty thus defined underlies twentieth century democracy. Liberty thus defined exists in a large part of the western world. And even where this equal right of all has not yet been accepted as a political right, its ethical value is becoming recognized.[63]

*

Liberty is the greatest developer. Herodotus tells us that while the tyrants ruled, the Athenians were no better fighters than their neighbors; but when freed they immediately surpassed all others.[64]

*

Liberty has knit us closely together as Americans.[65]

[62] See Employers and Unions.
[63] See Individuality of Peoples.
[64] See Industrial Democracy.
[65] See E Pluribus Unum.

LIBERTY'S GREATEST DANGER

The greatest dangers to liberty lurk in insidious encroachment by men of zeal, well-meaning but without understanding.[66]

LIBERTY THROUGH LAW

The great achievement of the English-speaking people is the attainment of liberty through law.

LIBRARY

[270] The library was to be not a static thing, but a dynamic force.

LIQUOR

The use of liquor is not a wrong. It is the abuse and not the use which is wrong. . . . Remember the weaknesses of men and endeavor to protect them but do not forget that even the weak are strong enough to resist too severe restrictions. Remember that any regulations which you may adopt will, at best, *reduce* the evil which is sure to flow from the appetite of men for stimulating liquors.

LIVING LAW [67]

The Struggle Continues. The court reawakened to the truth of the old maxim of the civilians, *Ex facto jus oritur.* It realized that no law, written or unwritten, can be understood without a full knowledge of the facts out of which it is to be applied. But the struggle for the living law has not been fully won.

LOGIC OF REALITIES [68]

The logic of words should yield to the logic of realities.

---

[66] See Government Intrusion.
[67] See also Law and Life.
[68] See also Facts.

LONG HOURS[69]

The first question in considering the condition of labor
is, and to my mind must be, the hours of labor. No matter
what men are paid, no matter what the ordinary conditions
may be under which they work, the first question must be,
How long did this man work? Because not only does the
excess of hours of labor entail upon the individual very
serious consequences in respect to health and the ability to
endure labor in the future, but the effect upon the community as a whole is of infinite importance; in the first
place, in determining what is the time that is left to the
individual to devote himself to the needs of his own family,
to aid in the education and the bringing up of his children;
and in the second place, what is the time that is left to the
individual to perform those duties which are incumbent
upon him as a citizen of a free country.

*

[275] The best of wages will not compensate for excess-
ively long working hours which undermine health.

*

The effect of overwork on morals is closely related to the
injury of health. Laxity of moral fibre follows physical de-
bility. When the working day is so long that no time whatever is left for a minimum of leisure or home life, relief
from the strain of work is sought in alcoholic stimulants and
other excesses.   *

The fatigue which follows long hours of labor becomes
chronic and results in general deterioration of health. Often
ignored, since it does not result in immediate disease, this
weakness and anaemia undermines the whole system; it
destroys the nervous energy most necessary for steady work,
and effectually predisposes to other illness. The long hours

---

[69] See also Leisure, Short Workday.

of standing, which are required in many industries, are universally denounced by physicians as the cause of pelvic disorders.

LOW WAGES

No proposition in economics is better established than that low wages are not cheap wages. On the contrary, the best in wages is the cheapest. . . . Why should the proposition be doubted, that wages insufficient to sustain the worker properly are uneconomical? Does anybody doubt that the only way you can get work out of a horse is to feed the horse properly? Does anyone doubt that the only way you can get hens to lay, is to feed the hens properly? Regarding cows we know now that even proper feeding is not enough, or proper material living conditions. . . . Experience has taught us that harsh language addressed to a cow impairs her usefulness. Are women less sensitive than beasts in these respects?

LOYALTY

The loyalty that you want is loyalty to the real employer, to the people of the United States. This idea that loyalty to an immediate superior is something commendable when it goes to a forgetfulness of one's country involves a strange misconception of what democracy is. It is a revival—a relic —of the slave status, a relic of the time when "the king could do no wrong," and when everybody owed allegiance to the king.

WM. H. MCELWAIN

[280]   He worked for nobler ends than mere accumulation or lust of power. . . . McElwain made so many advances in the methods and practices of the long-established and prosperous branch of industry in which he was engaged, that he may be said to have revolutionized shoe manufacturing. He found it a trade; he left it an applied science.

MACCABEAN STRUGGLE

As a part of the eternal world-wide struggle for democracy, the struggle of the Maccabees is of eternal world-wide interest. It is a struggle of the Jews today, as well as those of 2,000 years ago. It is a struggle of America as well as of Palestine. It is a struggle in which all Americans, non-Jews as well as Jews, should be vitally interested because they are vitally affected.

MACHINERY

The great advance created by the introduction of machinery we permitted, in large measure, to be dissipated socially—instead of utilizing the opportunity fully to raise the standard of our civilization.

MAIN FACTOR IN BETTERMENT

Seek for betterment within the broad lines of existing institutions. Do so by attacking evil *in situ*; and proceed from the individual to the general. Remember that progress is necessarily slow; that remedies are necessarily tentative; that because of varying conditions there must be much and constant enquiry into facts . . . and much experimentation; and that always and everywhere the intellectual, moral and spiritual development of those concerned will remain an essential—and the main factor—in real betterment.[70]

MAN

Men are not bad, men are not degraded, because they desire to be so; they are degraded largely through circumstances.

*

[285]   Man is weak and his judgment is at best fallible.[71]

---

[70] See Existing Institutions.
[71] See Experimentation.

*
Man has not kept pace in growth with his works.

MAN'S WORK

Man's work is, at best, so insignificant compared with that of the Creator—it is all so Lilliputian, one cannot bow before it.[72]

MASSACHUSETTS' TASK

No one but a fanatic can be *sure* that his opinions—political, economic, or social—are correct. But no man, be he reactionary or progressive, ought to doubt that free thought and free speech are necessary in a democracy; and that their exercise in things public should be encouraged. My opponents throughout long years practically refused to discuss publicly or privately with me the measures under consideration. For opposing arguments they substituted attacks upon reputation. And the community permitted them to do so almost without a protest. This seems to me the fundamental defect. Our task in Massachusetts is to reconstruct manhood.

MESSIAH

The belief in a Messiah and a Messianic Age is foreign to my way of thinking. My interests are the real, natural, and intelligible, and also the probable and possible. I hold it to be improbable and impossible that there will ever live a man who will possess all knowledge and be in a position to solve all of man's problems, or that there will come an age that will be altogether free from trouble and vexation. As to whether the belief in a Messiah has been helpful or harmful I cannot say. Certain socialist thinkers have maintained that it has hindered progress. But I doubt it. No one has as yet proved satisfactorily whether the acceptance of

---

[72] See Character.

dogmas affects a man's conduct one way or another. My
impression is that the faithful outnumber the virtuous and
that not all the unbelieving are saints.

MINIMUM WAGE

[290]   I am convinced that a minimum wage instead of
adding to the expense of an establishment would, after the
initial period of introduction, reduce the actual expenses
of the establishment. Anything which is of better quality,
which costs a little more, gives a larger percentage of value
than the thing that is cheap. It is one of the curses of the
poor that they have to buy poor things; and it is precisely
the same in regard to human labor and human service as
in regard to merchandise.

MIRACLES

There has been more nonsense written about miracles
than almost about any other subject. On the whole I gather
the impression that those who loudly protest their belief
in miracles feel the need of reassuring themselves.

MONEY

The service of money will resemble that of water in agriculture—always indispensable, always beneficent to the point
where it becomes excessive but of little avail unless the soil
be rich, naturally or through fertilizers, unless there be
appropriate cultivation, and unless the operations be conducted with good judgment.

MONEY-MAKING AND SERVICE

Think of the great work that has been done in the world
by men who had no thought of money reward. No; money
is not worth a great man's time. It is unworthy of greatness
to strive for that alone. What then? Power? That isn't
much better, if you mean the kind of power that springs
from money. Is it the game? You hear that nowadays—

the game! It sounds too frivolous. To me the word is Service. Money-making will become incidental to Service. The man of the future will think more of giving Service than of making money, no matter what particular kind of Service it happens to be. It will become a distinction worth striving for to give the best Service, whether you are conducting a retail shop or a great railroad. It naturally follows that those who give the best Service will make money, because success must be profitable, yet Service, and not money-making, will be the end. Though the work of the greatest artists may command the highest prices, their incentive has not been money. It has been the desire to achieve professional success.[73] That will be the spirit of business in the future.[74]

MONOPOLY[75]

There are still intelligent, informed, just-minded and civilized persons who believe that the rapidly growing aggregation of capital through corporations constitutes an insidious menace to the liberty of the citizen; that it tends to increase the subjection of labor to capital; that, because of the guidance and control necessarily exercised by great corporations upon those engaged in business, individual initiative is being impaired and creative power will be lessened; that the absorption of capital by corporations, and their perpetual life, may bring evils similar to those which attended mortmain; that the evils incident to the accelerating absorption of business by corporations outweigh the benefits thereby secured; and that the process of absorption should be retarded.

---

[73] See Artists.
[74] See also Business—A Profession.
[75] See also Absolute Power, Bankers' Ethics, Industrial Absolutism, Industrial Liberty, People's Own Gold, Regulated Competition, Sherman Law, Socialism.

*

[295]   The assertion that the great financial interests exercise a potent, subtle, and sinister influence in the important decisions of our Government had often been made by men high in authority.

*

The prevalence of the corporation in America has led men of this generation to act, at times, as if the privilege of doing business in corporate form were inherent in the citizen; and has led them to accept the evils attendant upon the free and unrestricted use of the corporate mechanism as if these evils were the inescapable price of civilized life, and, hence, to be borne with resignation. Throughout the greater part of our history a different view prevailed.

*

Size alone gives to giant corporations a social significance not attached ordinarily to smaller units of private enterprise. Through size, corporations . . . are sometimes able to dominate the state. The typical business corporation of the last century, owned by a small group of individuals, managed by their owners, and limited in size by their personal wealth, is being supplanted by huge concerns in which the lives of tens or hundreds of thousands of investors are subjected, through the corporate mechanism, to the control of a few men. Ownership has been separated from control; and this separation has removed many of the checks which formerly operated to curb the misuse of wealth and power. And as ownership of the shares is becoming continually more dispersed, the power which formerly accompanied ownership is becoming increasingly concentrated in the hands of a few. The changes thereby wrought in the lives of the workers, of the owners, and of the general public, are so fundamental and far-reaching as to lead these scholars to compare the evolving "corporate system" with the feudal system; and to lead other men of insight and experience to assert that this "master institution of civilized life" is committing it to the rule of a plutocracy.

*

The statement that size is not a crime is entirely correct when you speak of it from the point of motive. But size may become such a danger in its results to the community that the community may have to set limits. A large part of our protective legislation consists of prohibiting things which we find are dangerous, according to common experience. Concentration of power has been shown to be dangerous in a democracy, even though that power may be used beneficently.[76]

*

The trust problem can never be settled right for the American people by looking at it through the spectacles of bonds and stocks. You must study it through the spectacles of people's rights and people's interests; must consider the effect upon the development of the American democracy. When you do that you will realize the extraordinary perils to our institutions which attend the trusts; you will realize the danger of letting the people learn that our sacred Constitution protects not only vested rights but vested wrongs. The situation is a very serious one; unless wise legislation is enacted we shall have as a result of that social unrest, a condition which will be more serious than that produced by the fall of a few points in stock-exchange quotations.

*

[300] The first essential of wise and just action is knowledge. And as a means of obtaining this knowledge we should secure uniform account. It was, as I remember, the great Colbert who said, "Accountancy—that is government."

[76] See also Big Business, Bigness.

*

Nobody can form a judgment that is worth having without a fairly detailed and intimate knowledge of the facts, and the circumstances of these gentlemen, largely bankers of importance, with a multitude of different associations and occupations—the fact that those men cannot know the facts is conclusive to my mind against a system by which the same men are directors in many different companies. I doubt whether anybody who is himself engaged in any important business has time to be a director in more than one large corporation. If he seeks to know about the affairs of that one corporation as much as he should know, not only in the interest of the stockholders, but in the interest of the community, he will have a field for study that will certainly occupy all the time that he has.[77]

*

My observation leads me to believe that while there are many contributing causes to unrest, there is one cause which is fundamental. That is the necessary conflict—the contrast between our political liberty and our industrial absolutism.[78] We are as free politically, perhaps, as free as it is possible for us to be. Every male has his voice and vote; and the law has endeavored to enable, and has succeeded practically, in enabling him to exercise his political franchise without fear. He therefore has his part; and certainly can secure an adequate part in the government of the country in all of its political relations; that is, in all relations which are determined directly by legislation or governmental administration.

On the other hand, in dealing with industrial problems the position of the ordinary worker is exactly the reverse. The individual employee has no effective voice or vote. And

[77] See also Concentration, Interlocking Directorates, Joiners.
[78] Repeated under Unrest.

the main objection, as I see it, to the very large corporation is, that it makes possible—and in many cases makes inevitable—the exercise of industrial absolutism. It is not merely the case of the individual worker against the employer which, even if he is a reasonably sized employer, presents a serious situation calling for the interposition of a union to protect the individual. But we have the situation of an employer so potent, so well organized, with such concentrated forces and with such extraordinary powers of reserve and the ability to endure against strikes and other efforts of a union, that the relatively loosely organized masses of even strong unions are unable to cope with the situation. We are dealing here with a question, not of motive, but of condition. Now, the large corporations and the managers of the powerful corporations are probably in large part actuated by motives just the same as an employer of a tenth of their size. Neither of them, as a rule, wishes to have his liberty abridged; but the smaller concern usually comes to the conclusion that it is necessary that it should be, where an important union must be dealt with. But when a great financial power has developed—when there exist these powerful organizations, which can successfully summon forces from all parts of the country, which can afford to use tremendous amounts of money in any conflict to carry out what they deem to be their business principle, and can also afford to suffer large losses—you have necessarily a condition of inequality between the two contending forces. Such contests, though undertaken with the best motives and with strong conviction on the part of the corporate managers that they are seeking what is for the best interests not only of the company but of the community, lead to absolutism. The result, in the cases of these large corporations, may be to develop a benevolent absolutism, but it is an absolutism all the same; and it is that which makes the great corporation so dangerous. There develops within the State a state so powerful that the ordinary social and industrial forces existing are insufficient to cope with it.

*

Many dangers to democracy . . . are inherent in these huge aggregations.[79]

*

All the power of capital and all the ability and intelligence of the men who wield and who serve the capital have been used to make practically slaves of these operatives, because it does not mean merely in respect to the way in which they have lived, but the very worst part of all this is the repression. It is a condition of repression, of slavery in the real sense of the word, which is alien to American conditions.

*

[305] More serious . . . is the effect of the Money Trust in directly suppressing competition. That suppression enables the monopolist to extort excessive profits; but monopoly increases the burden of the consumer even more in other ways. Monopoly arrests development; and through arresting development, prevents that lessening of the cost of production and of distribution which would otherwise take place. . . .

But far more serious even than the suppression of competition is the suppression of industrial liberty, indeed of manhood itself, which this overweening financial power entails. The intimidation which it effects extends far beyond "the banks, trust companies, and other institutions seeking participation from this inner group in their lucrative underwritings"; and far beyond those interested in the great corporations directly dependent upon the inner group. Its blighting and benumbing effect extends as well to the small and seemingly independent business man, to the vast army

---

[79] See Dangers to Democracy.

of professional men and others directly dependent upon "Big Business," and to many another.

*

The talk of the agitator alone does not advance socialism a step; but the formation of great trusts—the huge railroad consolidations—the insurance "racers" with the attendant rapacity or the dishonesty of their potent managers, and their frequent corruption of councils and legislatures is hastening us almost irresistibly into socialistic measures. The great captains of industry and of finance, who profess the greatest horror of the extension of governmental functions, are the chief makers of socialism. Socialistic thinkers smile approvingly at the operations of Morgan, Perkins and Rockefeller, and of the Hydes, McCalls and McCurdys. They see approaching the glad day when monopoly shall have brought all industry and finance under a single head, so that with the cutting of a single neck, as Nero vainly wished for his Christian subjects, destruction of the enemy may be accomplished. Our great trust-building, trust-abusing capitalists have in their selfish shortsightedness become the makers of socialism, proclaiming by their acts, like the nobles of France, "After us, The Deluge!" [80]

*

It has been suggested that we accept the proposed monopoly in transportation but provide safeguards.

This would be like surrendering liberty and substituting despotism with safeguards. There is no way in which to safeguard people from despotism except to prevent despotism.[81] There is no way to safeguard the people from the evils of a private transportation monopoly except to prevent the monopoly. The objections to despotism and to monopoly are fundamental in human nature. They rest upon the

---

[80] Repeated under Socialism.
[81] See Despotism.

innate and ineradicable selfishness of man. They rest upon
the fact that absolute power inevitably leads to abuse. They
rest upon the fact that progress flows only from struggle.[82]

*

We have got to encourage in every way the individual
enterprise, and we have to bear in mind that on the one
hand while you are encouraging the enterprise and making
for the advance of the country and the prosperity of the
individual, the inventor, and the business man; on the other
hand, the moment you get these large organizations, these
large trusts, you are doing exactly the opposite; you are putting an actual damper upon advance.

*

Human nature is such that monopolies, however well intentioned and however well regulated, inevitably become
oppressive, arbitrary, unprogressive and inefficient.[83]

*

[310]   We have no place in the American democracy for
the money king, not even for the merchant prince. We are
confronted in the twentieth century, as we were in the nineteenth century, with an irreconcilable conflict. Our democracy cannot endure half free and half slave. The essence of
the trust is a combination of the capitalist, by the capitalist, for the capitalist.[84]

*

The American people have as little need of oligarchy in
business as in politics.

*

We must break the Money Trust or the Money Trust
will break us.

---

[82] Repeated under Progress.
[83] See Human Nature.
[84] See Half Free and Half Slave.

MONOPOLY AND EFFICIENCY

Whenever trusts have developed efficiency, their fruits have been absorbed almost wholly by the trusts themselves. From such efficiency as they have developed, the community has gained substantially nothing.

*

It is true that the unit in business may be too small to be efficient. It is also true that the unit may be too large to be efficient, and this is no uncommon incident of monopoly.[85]

MOTIVES AND RESULTS

[315]   In things economic and social, wrong results do not proceed to any very great extent from wrong motives. The motives are, in the main, right—meaning by "motives," intent. But the results sought are very often wrong. People fail to recognize true values. It is failure to recognize things at their real worth which leads to unfortunate results.

NATIONAL INDIVIDUALITY

The movements of the last century have proved that whole peoples have individuality no less marked than that of the single person; that the individuality of a people is irrepressible, and that the misnamed internationalism which seeks the obliteration of nationalities or peoples is unattainable.[85a] The new nationalism adopted by America proclaims that each race or people, like each individual, has the right and duty to develop, and that only through such differentiated development will high civilization be attained. Not until these principles of nationalism, like those of democracy, are generally accepted will liberty be fully attained and minorities be secure in their rights. Not until then can the foundation be laid for a lasting peace among the nations.

---

[85] See also Efficiency.
[85a] See also Individuality of Peoples, Jewish Individuality.

NATIONALITY

Deeply imbedded in every people is the desire for full development, the longing, as Mazzini phrased it, "to elaborate and express their idea, to contribute their stone also to the pyramid of history." Nationality like democracy has been one of the potent forces making for man's advance during the past hundred years. The assertion of nationality has infused whole peoples with hope, manhood and self-respect. It has ennobled and made purposeful millions of lives. It offered them a future, and in doing so revived and capitalized all that was valuable in their past. The assertion of nationality raised Ireland from the slough of despondency. It roused Southern Slavs to heroic deeds. It created gallant Belgium. It freed Greece. It gave us united Italy. It manifested itself even among the free peoples, like the Welsh, who had no grievance, but who gave expression to their nationality through the revival of the old Cymric tongue. Each of these peoples developed because, as Mazzini said, they were enabled to proclaim "to the world that they also live, think, love, and labor for the benefit of all." [86]

NATION AND NATIONALITY

The difference between a nation and a nationality is clear; but it is not always observed. Likeness between members is the essence of nationality; but the members of a nation may be very different. A nation may be composed of many nationalities, as some of the most successful nations are. An instance of this is the British nation, with its division into English, Scotch, Welsh, and Irish at home; with the French in Canada; and throughout the Empire, scores of other nationalities. Other examples are furnished by the Swiss nation with its German, French, and Italian sections; by the Belgian nation composed of Flemings and Walloons; and by the American nation which comprises nearly all the

[86] See also Individuality of Peoples, Jewish Individuality.

white nationalities. The unity of a nationality is a fact of nature; the unification into a nation is largely the work of man. The false doctrine that nation and nationality must be made coextensive is the cause of some of our greatest tragedies. It is, in large part, the cause also of the present war.[87] It has led, on the one hand, to cruel, futile attempts at enforced assimilation, like the Russianizing of Finland and Poland, and the Prussianizing of Posen, Schleswig-Holstein, and Alsace-Lorraine. It has led, on the other hand, to those Panistic movements which are a cloak for territorial ambitions. As a nation may develop though composed of many nationalities, so a nationality may develop though forming parts of several nations. The essential in either case is recognition of the equal rights of each nationality.

NATURE OF LAW

Few laws are of universal application. It is the nature of our law that it has dealt, not with man in general, but with him in relationship.

NEUTRALITY

[320] Neutrality is at times a graver sin than belligerence.[88]

NEW DEMANDS FOR JUSTICE

The great development of agencies now furnishing country-wide distribution of news, the vastness of our territory, and improvements in the means of transmitting intelligence, have made it possible for a news agency or newspapers to obtain, without paying compensation, the fruit of another's efforts and to use news so obtained gainfully in competition with the original collector. The injustice of such action is obvious. But to give relief against it would involve more than the application of existing rules of law to new facts. It would require the making of a new rule in anal-

---

[87] World War I.
[88] See Chosen People.

ogy to existing ones. The unwritten law possesses capacity for growth; and has often satisfied new demands for justice by invoking analogies or by expanding a rule or principle. This process has been in the main wisely applied and should not be discontinued. Where the problem is relatively simple, as it is apt to be when private interests only are involved, it generally proves adequate. But with the increasing complexity of society, the public interest tends to become omnipresent; and the problems presented by new demands for justice cease to be simple. Then the creation or recognition by courts of a new private right may work serious injury to the general public; unless the boundaries of the right are definitely established and wisely guarded. In order to reconcile the new private right with the public interest, it may be necessary to prescribe limitations and rules for its enjoyment; and also to provide administrative machinery for enforcing the rules. It is largely for this reason that, in the effort to meet the many new demands for justice incident to a rapidly changing civilization, resort to legislation has latterly been had with increasing frequency.

NEW FREEDOM

Break the control . . . exercised by the investment bankers over railroads, public-service, and industrial corporations, over banks, life insurance and trust companies, and a long step will have been taken toward attainment of the New Freedom.[89]   *

Give men a free field. Provide equality of opportunity and we attain the New Freedom.[90]

NOBLESSE OBLIGE

We have also an immediate and more pressing duty in the performance of which Zionism alone seems capable of af-

[89] See Interlocking Directorates.
[90] See Equality of Opportunity.

fording effective aid. We must protect America and ourselves from demoralization, which has to some extent already set in among American Jews. The cause of this demoralization is clear. It results in large part from the fact that in our land of liberty all the restraints by which the Jews were protected in their Ghettos were removed and a new generation left without necessary moral and spiritual support. And is it not equally clear what the only possible remedy is? It is the laborious task of inculcating self-respect, a task which can be accomplished only by restoring the ties of the Jew to the noble past of his race, and by making him realize the possibilities of a no less glorious future. The sole bulwark against demoralization is to develop in each new generation of Jews in America the sense of *noblesse oblige*. That spirit can be developed in those who regard their people as destined to live and to live with a bright future. That spirit can best be developed by actively participating in some way in furthering the ideals of the Jewish renaissance; and this can be done effectively only through furthering the Zionist movement.[91]

ONE LIFE TO LIVE

[325]   I have only one life to live and it's short enough. Why waste it on things that I don't want most? And I don't want money or property most. I want to be free.

ONE MASTER ONLY

There is great strength in serving with singleness of purpose one master only.

OPEN OPPORTUNITY

What America needs is not that we do anything for these, our fellow citizens, but that we keep open the path of opportunity to enable them to do for themselves.

---

[91] See also American Jewish Community, Zionism.

ORGANIZATION

Man's work often outruns the capacity of the individual man; and no matter how good the organization, the capacity of an individual man usually determines the success or failure of a particular enterprise—not only financially to the owners but in service to the community. Organization can do much to make concerns more efficient. Organization can do much to make larger units possible and profitable. But the efficacy even of organization has its bounds. There is a point where the centrifugal force necessarily exceeds the centripetal. And organization can never supply the combined judgment, initiative, enterprise and authority which must come from the chief executive officer. Nature sets a limit to his possible achievement.[92]

*

Organization can never be a substitute for initiative and for judgment.[93]

OUR NEW PEONAGE

[330]   Half a century ago nearly every American boy could look forward to becoming independent as a farmer or mechanic, in business or in professional life; and nearly every American girl might expect to become the wife of such a man. Today most American boys have reason to believe that throughout life they will work in some capacity as employees of others, either in private or public business; and a large percentage of the women occupy like positions. This revolutionary change has resulted from the growth of manufacturing and mining as compared with farming; from the formation of trusts and other large business corporations; from the marked increase in governmental functions; and finally, from the invasion of women into industry.

92 See also Bigness.
93 See Capacity of Individual Man.

PALESTINE

The land is an inspiration to effort. It is an inspiration not only because of its past and its associations, but because the present urges one on to make it bloom again—bloom, not only physically, but spiritually.

PARAMOUNT PUBLIC NEED

What, at any particular time, is the paramount public need is, necessarily, largely a matter of judgment. Hence, in passing upon the validity of a law challenged as being unreasonable, aid may be derived from the experience of other countries and of the several states of our Union in which the common law and its conceptions of liberty and of property prevail.

PARENTAGE

The greatest combination of good fortune any man can have is a parentage unusual for both brains and character.

PAST

The past is valuable as the mirror of the future.

PAST LOSSES

[335] Past losses obviously do not tend to prove present values. The fact that a sometime losing business becomes profitable eventually through growth of the community or more efficient management, tends to prove merely that the adventure was not wholly misconceived.

PATH TO BANKRUPTCY

The manufacturer who fails to recognize fire insurance, depreciation, interest and taxes as current charges of the business treads the path to bankruptcy. And that nation does the like which fails to recognize and provide against the economic, social and political conditions which impose upon the workingman so large a degree of financial dependence.

PEOPLE AND RAW MATERIAL

When we come to think about it hard, and really try, how much more rapidly we shall be able to produce results with people than from any other form of raw material. All the raw material from which man produces his mechanical miracles is inert. But the people, as raw material, can help. They have will.

PEOPLE AND RICH

Every act of injustice on the part of the rich will be met by another act or many acts of injustice on the part of the people.[94]

PEOPLE'S OWN GOLD

The goose that lays golden eggs has been considered a most valuable possession. But even more profitable is the privilege of taking the golden eggs laid by somebody else's goose. The investment bankers and their associates now enjoy that privilege. They control the people through the people's own money. If the bankers' power were commensurate only with their wealth, they would have relatively little influence on American business. Vast fortunes like those of the Astors are no doubt regrettable. They are inconsistent with democracy. They are unsocial. And they seem peculiarly unjust when they represent largely unearned increment. But the wealth of the Astors does not endanger political or industrial liberty. It is insignificant in amount as compared with the aggregate wealth of America, or even of New York City. It lacks significance largely because its owners have only the income from their own wealth. The Astor wealth is static. The wealth of the Morgan associates is dynamic. The power and the growth of power of our financial oligarchs

[94] See Excesses of Capital.

comes from wielding the savings and quick capital of others. In two of the three great life insurance companies the influence of J. P. Morgan & Co. and their associates is exerted without any individual investment by them whatsoever. Even in the Equitable, where Mr. Morgan bought an actual majority of all the outstanding stock, his investment amounts to little more than one-half of one per cent. of the assets of the company. The fetters which bind the people are forged from the people's own gold.[95]

POLITICIAN

[340] The politician can stand any amount of attack, but he cannot stand the opposition of public opinion. We cannot submit to the dishonor of being represented by those men. We should not allow ourselves to be represented by thieves and convicts.

POPULAR OPINION

My early associations were such as to give me greater reverence than I now have for the things that are because they are. I recall that when I began to practice law I thought it awkward, stupid, and vulgar that a jury of twelve inexpert men should have the power to decide. I had the greatest respect for the Judge. I trusted only expert opinion. Experience of life has made me democratic. I began to see that many things sanctioned by expert opinion and denounced by popular opinion were wrong.

POSSIBILITIES OF HUMAN DEVELOPMENT

I believe that the possibilities of human advancement are unlimited. I believe that the resources of productive enterprise are almost untouched, and that the world will see a vastly increased supply of comforts, a tremendous social surplus out of which the great masses will be apportioned a degree of well-being that is now hardly dreamed of.

---

[95] See also Banker-Middleman, Monopoly.

PRACTICAL MEN

Theoreticians are signposts, but the distances between them are often best transversed by practical men.

PREPAREDNESS

"Preparedness" implies far more than adequate military equipment and training. It implies conservation and development of all the resources of the nation, human and material. It implies that in industry and in agriculture there will be constant effort to improve the methods and means of production and distribution. It implies that men and women will be trained for the vocations they are to pursue, and that opportunity shall exist to make their labor effective. It implies that conditions of living, as of work, shall be such that every American citizen may, throughout life, be fit to perform the duties of citizenship, and that he may, by participation in its privileges, learn to understand American ideals and become eager to cooperate for their attainment.

PRICE CONTROL

[345] The denial of the right to establish standard prices results in granting a privilege to the big concerns; a discrimination in favor of the rich and powerful as against the small man; for the concern with large capital, as the powerful trusts, can secure adherence to the standard price while the small manufacturer or producer can not. The small man needs the protection of the law; but the law becomes the instrument by which he is destroyed.

PRIVATE CITIZEN

The most important office and the one which all of us can and should fill is that of private citizen. The duties of the office of private citizen cannot under a republican form of government be neglected without serious injury to the public.

PRODUCTION

It is one of the greatest economic errors to put any limitation upon production.

PRODUCTS OF THE MIND

The fact that a product of the mind has cost its producer money and labor, and has a value for which others are willing to pay, is not sufficient to ensure to it this legal attribute of property. The general rule of law is, that the noblest of human productions—knowledge, truths ascertained, conceptions, and ideas—become, after voluntary communication to others, free as the air to common use. Upon these incorporeal productions the attribute of property is continued after such communication only in certain classes of cases where public policy has seemed to demand it. These exceptions are confined to productions which, in some degree, involve creation, invention, or discovery. But by no means all such are endowed with this attribute of property.

PROFIT SHARING

To a greater or less extent in small business the owners are beginning to recognize that there is but one principle by which lasting success can be attained, and it is this: Those who do the work shall get in some fair proportion what they produce. The share to which capital as such is entitled is small. All the rest should go to those, high and low, who do the work.

PROGRESS

[350] Progress flows only from struggle.[96]

PROPER CONFERENCES

Nine-tenths of the serious controversies which arise in life result from misunderstanding, result from one man not knowing the facts which to the other man seem important,

---

[96] See Monopoly.

or otherwise failing to appreciate his point of view. A properly conducted conference involves a frank disclosure of such facts—patient, careful argument, willingness to listen and to consider.[97]

Bluff and bluster have no place there. The spirit must be, "Come, let us reason together." Such a conference is impossible where the employer clings to the archaic belief commonly expressed in the words, "This is my business, and I will run it as I please." It is impossible where the labor representative, swaggering in his power to inflict injury by strike and boycott, is seeking an unfair advantage of the employers, or would seek to maintain even a proper position by improper means. Such conferences will succeed only if employer and employee recognize that, even if there be no so-called system of profit-sharing, they are in a most important sense partners, and that each is entitled to a patient hearing, with a mind as open as the prejudice of self-interest permits.[98]

PROPERTY

Property must be subject to that control of property which is essential to the enjoyment by every man of a free individual life. And when property is used to interfere with that fundamental freedom of life for which property is *only a means*, then property must be controlled. This applies to the regulation of trusts and railroads, public utilities and all the big industries that control the necessities of life. Laws regulating them, far from being infringements on liberty, are in reality protections against infringements on liberty.

*

Property is only a means. It has been a frequent error of our courts that they have made the means an end. Once correct that error, put property back into its right place,

[97] Repeated under Employer and Employee, Serious Controversies.
[98] See Employer and Employee.

and the whole social-legal conception becomes at once consistent.

PROPRIETY

To publish of a modest and retiring individual that he suffers from an impediment in his speech or that he cannot spell correctly, is an unwarranted, if not an unexampled, infringement of his rights, while to state and comment on the same characteristics found in a would-be congressman could not be regarded as beyond the pale of propriety.[99]

PUBLIC INTERESTS

[355] Private interests will always be and should properly be active in presenting to legislators what they deem to be required for the protection of the enterprises they represent. But it is essential to just and safe legislation that the interests of the public should also be specifically and ably represented.

PUBLICITY

Publicity is justly commended as a remedy for social and industrial diseases. Sunlight is said to be the best of disinfectants; electric light the most efficient policeman.

PUBLIC OPINION

We need intelligent public opinion. I don't mean the periodic, spasmodic indignation at wrong. That won't give us good government. It is necessary to force the people to think of this corruption and the great need of action for the public good.

PUBLIC SERVICE

Some men buy diamonds and rare works of art. Others delight in autos and yachts. My luxury is to invest my surplus effort, beyond that required for the proper support of

[99] See also Blighting Influence of Journalistic Gossip.

my family, to the pleasure of taking up a public problem and solving, or helping to solve, it for the people without receiving any compensation. Your yachtsman or automobilist would lose much of his enjoyment if he were obliged to do for pay what he is doing for the love of the thing itself. So I should lose much of my satisfaction if I were paid in connection with public services of this kind.

PUNCTUALITY

Generally speaking I should say that a human being who cannot organize himself so as to keep his appointments on time is an unorganized human being. And I do not believe that anybody or anything is at his best when in a state of disorganization. People think that poets and philosophers are notoriously absent-minded, forgetful, and disarranged. Well they may be absent-minded and forgetful, but not disarranged. There is a pattern of organization in Dante's *Divine Comedy* and Kant's *Critique of Pure Reason* which any construction engineer might envy and emulate.

PURITANS

[360]   Democratic ideals cannot be attained through emphasis merely upon the rights of man. Even a recognition that every right has a correlative duty will not meet the needs of democracy. Duty must be accepted as the dominant conception in life. Such were the conditions in the early days of the Colonies and states of New England, when American democracy reached there its fullest expression; for the Puritans were trained in implicit obedience to stern duty by constant study of the Prophets.[1]

QUALITY AND SPIRITUAL VALUE

The growth of the future—at least of the immediate future—must be in quality and spiritual value.[2]

---

[1] See Jews and Democracy.
[2] Repeated under Small Groups.

RADICALS AND CONSERVATIVES

Radicals who would take us back to the roots of things often fail because they disregard the fruit Time has produced and preserved. Conservatives fail because they would preserve even what Time has decomposed.

RATE-MAKING

The expense and loss now incident to recurrent rate controversies is also very large. The most serious vice of the present rule for fixing the rate base is not the existing uncertainty; but that the method does not lead to certainty. Under it, the value for rate-making purposes must ever be an unstable factor. Instability is a standing menace of renewed controversy. The direct expense to the utility of maintaining an army of experts and of counsel is appalling. The indirect cost is far greater. The attention of officials high and low is, necessarily, diverted from the constructive tasks of efficient operation and of development. The public relations of the utility to the community are apt to become more and more strained. And a victory for the utility may, in the end, prove more disastrous than defeat would have been. The community defeated, but unconvinced, remembers; and may refuse aid when the company has occasion later to require its consent or cooperation in the conduct and development of its enterprise. Controversy with utilities is obviously injurious also to the public interest. The prime needs of the community are that facilities be ample and that rates be as low and as stable as possible. The community can get cheap service from private companies only through cheap capital. It can get efficient service only if managers of the utility are free to devote themselves to problems of operation and of development. It can get ample service through private companies only if investors may be assured of receiving continuously a fair return upon the investment.

READING

Remember that even if you are able to read a good book and understand it, even this is not all; you must think of it after you have ceased reading, and not allow your mind to be immediately taken up by your own little petty affairs the moment you set the book aside. To profit by what you read not only concentration of mind is necessary *whilst* reading but *after thought*.

REGULATED COMPETITION

[365]   Shall we abandon as obsolete the long-cherished policy of competition, and accept in its place the long-detested policy of monopoly? The issue is not (as it is usually stated by advocates of monopoly), "Shall we have unrestricted competition or regulated monopoly?" It is "Shall we have regulated competition or regulated monopoly?"

Regulation is essential to the preservation and development of competition, just as it is necessary to the preservation and best development of liberty. We have long curbed the physically strong, to protect those physically weaker. More recently we have extended such prohibitions to business. We have restricted theoretical freedom of contract by factory laws. The liberty of the merchant and manufacturer to lie in trade, expressed in the fine phrase of *caveat emptor*, is yielding to the better conceptions of business ethics, before pure-food laws and postal-fraud prosecutions. Similarly, the right to competition must be limited in order to preserve it. For excesses of competition lead to monopoly, as excesses of liberty lead to absolutism. The extremes meet.[3]

The issue, therefore, is: Regulated competition *versus* regulated monopoly. The policy of regulated competition is distinctly a constructive policy. It is the policy of develop-

---

[3] See Excesses.

ment as distinguished from the destructive policy of private monopoly.[4]

REGULATION

The policy of regulating public-service companies is sound, but it must not be overworked. The scope of any possible effective regulation of an interstate railroad, either by Federal or by State commissions, is limited to a relatively narrow sphere. Regulation may prevent positive abuses, like discriminations, or excessive rates. Regulation may prevent persistent disregard of definite public demands, like that for specific trains or for stops at certain stations. Regulation may compel the correction of definite evils, like the use of unsanitary cars. But regulation cannot make inefficient business efficient. Regulation cannot convert a poorly managed railroad into a well-managed railroad. Regulation cannot supply initiative or energy. Regulation cannot infuse into railroad executives the will to please the people. Regulation cannot overcome the anaemia or wasting-sickness which attends monopoly. Regulation may curb, but it cannot develop the action of railroad officials.

REMEDIAL INSTITUTIONS

Refuse to accept as inevitable any evil in business (*i.e.,* irregularity of employment). Refuse to tolerate any immoral practice (*e.g.,* espionage). But do not believe that you can find a universal remedy for evil conditions or immoral practices in effecting a fundamental change in society (as by State Socialism).[5] And do not pin too much faith in legislation. Remedial institutions are apt to fall under the control of the enemy and to become instruments of oppression.[6]

[4] See also Competition, Monopoly.
[5] Repeated under Socialism.
[6] See also Socialism.

RESETTLEMENT OF PALESTINE

Palestine is being resettled by Jews. The resettlement has been largely the result of deliberate plans carried out through collective action. Men have differed concerning the wisdom of the Zionist movement. Men differ still in their predictions as to its results. But there is substantial agreement, among Jews and among non-Jews, that the resettlement is an event of historic significance. To students of history the subject is one of special interest because of the nature of the problem and the means employed.

RESPONSIBILITY

The great developer is responsibility. Hence no remedy can be hopeful which does not devolve upon the workers participation in responsibility for the conduct of business; and their aim should be the eventual assumption of full responsibility—as in cooperative enterprises. This participation in and eventual control of industry is likewise an essential of obtaining justice in distributing the fruits of industry.[7]

RESURRECTION

[370] Resurrection is a dogma, if it is that, that I should rather not discuss. I know how we love our precious little body, how much attentions some bestow upon it, and how loath we are to part from it, if part we do. I am not unacquainted with the weakness of man and his conceitedness, and I can understand that in the infancy of the race he was impelled to mistake death for a long sleep. But that human beings should be under the illusion to this day attests both the deep darkness in the human mind and the failure of education and science. Of all the crude beliefs which we inherited from the past I regard this one as the least worthy of the Jewish people. There is no reason why a Jew who be-

---

[7] See also Labor's Share.

lieves in the resurrection of the dead should not also believe in devils and angels, and in magic and astrology as well.

REVELATION

I have never been able to find out what the theologians mean by revelation. The Biblical account of what happened on Mount Sinai I think I understand, for it is simple, naive, anthropomorphic, and primitive. In that account the distance between man and God vanishes. Moses and God are in close proximity. They are both on the top of the mountain, speak to each other, and together speak to the people. God's voice is quite naturally the stronger, more like a peal of thunder than a human voice, so much so that it terrifies the people.

But God speaks with a voice. And a voice implies organs producing it. That is, something material and tangible as is an image or a picture. True, in later ages, when the effort was made to establish the incorporeality of God as a dogma, Jews were urged to remember that they saw no picture at Sinai and had heard only a voice speaking from the midst of a fire. This, to my mind, means only that in those ages men were in a quandary. On the one hand they insisted that God was immaterial and on the other that He had communicated with man or could do so at His will. To extricate themselves from embarrassment various compromises were attempted. At first, man's sense of hearing was favored over against his sense of seeing, the act of hearing having been apparently regarded as supersensual, as was the act of speaking. Later "hearing" was replaced by thinking and feeling as induced by emanations from God.

I have not read much of the literature that I understand is extant on emanation or emanations. But from the little that I did read and from what I have gathered in conversation I am satisfied that the theologians have not been successful in bridging the gap between the insubstantial and the substantial. Nor, does it seem to me, have they gotten anywhere with their attempts to explain "thinking and feeling" as nonmaterial functions. If the body and brain do not do the thinking and feeling then I do not know what does.

The account of revelation on Sinai makes more sense. It is more "factual." That is, it records without sophistication what the people actually believed. It made God human. It located Him on a mountain and made Him speak and write, all as it did in the case of Moses. This is quite clear to me, and this is quite obviously a folktale as are many other Biblical accounts.

The theologians would get farther with most thinking men by acknowledging that these folktales are a strain on their faith than by rationalizing them into incomprehensibility.

Yes, I heard of "continued revelation." But what does it mean? Isn't it another attempt to conceal embarrassments? The theologian finds it extremely difficult to explain why God should have spoken to a few generations of men and then have stopped, particularly so since they cannot agree among themselves as to whom He spoke and what it was He really said. So they take their chance with continued revelation. But if God speaks today to all men as He did three thousand years ago to Moses then His speaking to Moses ceases to be unique or of any particular significance, and, it would seem to me, can no longer be set down as an article of faith.

I am impressed with the fact that the burden and content of the old revelations were legal codes. It proves that ancient man understood that but for law human society could not endure. But these legal codes certainly constitute no proof of revelation. In the first place, they suffer from very serious imperfections, from the imperfections to which all human efforts are subject. In the second place, the proponents of continued revelation are horrified at the suggestion that the Mesopotamian codes were revealed.

REVOLUTIONARY CHANGE

Revolutionary change in industrial control and management should be voluntary, not compulsory.

RIGHT TO PRIVACY

The protection of society must come mainly through a recognition of the rights of the individual. Each man is responsible for his own acts and omissions only. If he condones what he reprobates, with a weapon at hand equal to his defense, he is responsible for the results. If he resists, public opinion will rally to his support. Has he then such a weapon? It is believed that the common law provides him with one, forged in the slow fire of the centuries, and today fitly tempered to his hand. The common law has always recognized a man's house as his castle, impregnable, often even to its own officers engaged in the execution of its commands. Shall the courts thus close the front entrance to constituted authority, and open wide the back door to idle or prurient curiosity?[8]

RISKS

To take risks is the very essence of Jewish life, that is, to take necessary risks. The wise man seeks not to avoid but to minimize risks.

THEODORE ROOSEVELT AND WOODROW WILSON

[375]   President [Theodore] Roosevelt spoke forcefully and persuasively on liberal issues. President Wilson spoke logically and convincingly.

RULE OF LAW

It is usually more important that a rule of law be settled, than that it be settled right. Even where the error in declar-

---

[8] See also Blighting Influence of Journalistic Gossip

ing the rule is a matter of serious concern, it is ordinarily
better to seek correction by legislation.

SABBATH

In the home of my parents there was no Jewish Sabbath,
nor in my own home. But I recall vividly the joy and awe
with which my uncle, Lewis Dembitz, welcomed the arrival
of the day and the piety with which he observed it. I remember the extra delicacies, lighting of the candles, prayers over
a cup of wine, quaint chants, and Uncle Lewis poring over
books most of the day. I remember more particularly an
elusive something about him which was spoken of as the
"Sabbath peace" and which years later brought to my mind
a passage from Addison in which he speaks of stealing a day
out of life to live. That elusive something prevailed in many
a home in Boston on a Sunday and was not wanting at Harvard on the same day. Uncle Lewis used to say that he was
enjoying a foretaste of heaven. I used to think, and do so
now, that we need on earth the Jewish-Puritan Sabbath
without its oppressive restrictions.

SAVINGS BANK INSURANCE

What we want is to have the workingman free; not to
have him the beneficiary of a benevolent employer, and
freedom demands a development in the employees of that
self-control which results in thrift and in adequate provision
for the future. The development of our savings banks and
savings bank insurance will be effective in this direction.

SCIENTIFIC MANAGEMENT [9]

We hear a great deal about inequality in the distribution
of wealth or the profits of industry. Such inequality exists,
but it is clear that even if there were a perfectly fair distribution, our ideals could not be attained unless we succeeded
in greatly increasing the productivity of man. Perhaps the

---

[9] See also Efficiency.

greatest evil attendant upon this existing inequality is that it tends to discontent, which in turn discourages effort and therefore impairs productivity. Such progress as we have made in improving the condition of the workingmen during the last century, and particularly during the last fifty years, has been made possible by invention, by the introduction of machinery, through which the productivity of the individual man has been greatly increased. The misfortune is that when this method of increasing the productivity of man was introduced, labor did not get the share of the increased profit to which it was entitled. With the advent of the new science of management has come the next great opportunity for labor; and it seems to me of the utmost importance, not only that this science should be developed and should be applied as far as possible, but that it should be applied in cooperation with the representatives of organized labor, in order that labor may through this movement get its proper share in the proceeds of industry.

I take it that this science of management is nothing more than an organized effort, pursued intensively, to eliminate waste. The efficiency experts tell us how this may be done. The experts make the individual detailed study, which is an essential of the elimination of waste. But, after all, the fundamental problems are social and industrial. You cannot eliminate waste unless you secure the cooperation of the worker, and you cannot secure his cooperation unless he is satisfied that there is a fair distribution of profits.[10]

*

[380] Scientific management is merely an application to business of those methods which have been pursued in other branches of science, to discover the best and the most effective methods of accomplishing a result. Scientific management does not mean making men work harder. Its every

10 See also Labor's Share.

effort is to make them work less hard; to accomplish more
by the same amount of effort, and to eliminate all unnecessary motions; to educate them so as to make them more
effective; to give special assistance to those who when entering upon their work are most in need of assistance, because
they are least competent.

*

The great fact to remember is this. The coming *science of
management*, in this century, marks an advance comparable
only to that made by the coming of the *machine* in the last.
The profits from the machine were absorbed by capital. But
we have developed a social sense. And now of the profits
that are to come from the new scientific management, the
people are to have their share. These profits are to be immense. On our railroads alone at least a million dollars a day
might be saved by this kind of management. Not all the
material resources in our land can compare to this prodi-
gious field, the possibilities of the science which will increase
the efficiency of man. And *this* public domain must not be
preempted.[11]

SCIENTISTS AND THEOLOGIANS

The fellow scientist of a Newton has, as a rule, advanced
his findings. But theologians have altogether too often con-
fused and mystified the revelations of the great religious
teachers, and consequently retarded the good that those
revelations aimed to achieve.

SECURITIES

Among the most important facts to be learned for determining the real value of a security is the amount of water
it contains. And any excessive amount paid to the banker
for marketing a security is water.

---

[11] See also Efficiency.

SEPARATION OF GOVERNMENTAL POWERS

The development of our financial oligarchy followed, in this respect, lines with which the history of political despotism has familiarized us: usurpation, proceeding by gradual encroachment rather than by violent acts; subtle and often long-concealed concentration of distinct functions, which are beneficent when separately administered, and dangerous only when combined in the same persons. It was by processes such as these that Caesar Augustus became master of Rome. The makers of our own Constitution had in mind like dangers to our political liberty when they provided so carefully for the separation of governmental powers.

SERIOUS CONTROVERSIES

[385] Nine-tenths of the serious controversies which arise in life result from misunderstanding, result from one man not knowing the facts which to the other man seem important, or otherwise failing to appreciate his point of view. A properly conducted conference involves a frank disclosure of such facts—patient, careful argument, willingness to listen and to consider.[12]

SERVICE VS. CHARITY

The greatest happiness in life is not to donate but to serve.

SHERMAN LAW

The moment that you endeavor by a combination of superior power to close the field to competition or to restrict individual effort; the moment you take away from the people that protection which comes from the incentive in the individual to create, and from the opportunity of the customer to discriminate in his purchases (as you do when you close the avenues of competition)—then a grave danger arises to progress in industry and to the general welfare;

---

[12] See Employer and Employee, Proper Conferences.

and it is against such danger that the Sherman Law was appropriately directed. . . . It seeks to protect the small man against the powerful trust, against the capitalistic combination.

The Sherman Law seeks to protect men in the right freely to compete and to prevent practices which must result in suppressing competition. It seeks to preserve to the individual both the opportunity and the incentive to create, it seeks to encourage individual effort; and a right in the individual manufacturer of a competitive business to market his goods in his own way, by fixing, if he desires, the selling-price to the consumer, is in entire harmony with the underlying purposes of the Sherman Law. But when men combine to form a monopoly, or control a particular line or branch of trade, however good may be their intentions, they necessarily curb individual effort. Under the fundamental laws of human nature and of trade they withdraw incentive from those who enjoy the monopoly, and they narrow the field of human effort by confining leadership to a comparatively few individuals.

And even where a complete monopoly does not exist, a powerful combination makes it so difficult for others to enter the field that most men are practically barred by the great chances of failure from entering upon so unequal a contest. It is against such conditions that the Sherman Law was directed. That is, the true restraint of trade—restraint through monopoly or combinations tending to monopoly, a condition under which business success is at best temporary, is often delusive, and is always purchased at the expense of the community.[13]

SHORT CUTS

There are no short cuts in evolution.

---

[13] See also Competition, Monopoly.

SHORT WORKDAY[14]

History, which has illustrated the deterioration due to long hours, bears witness no less clearly to the regeneration due to the shorter working day. To the individual and to society alike, shorter hours have been a benefit wherever introduced. The married and unmarried working woman is enabled to obtain the decencies of life outside of working hours. With the improvement in home life, the tone of the entire community is raised.[15] Wherever sufficient time has elapsed since the establishment of the shorter working day, the succeeding generation has shown extraordinary improvement in physique and morals.

*

[390] The regulation of the working day has acted as a stimulus to improvement in the processes of manufacture. Invention of new machinery and perfection of old methods have followed the introduction of shorter hours.

*

To the preservation of freshness of mind a short workday is as essential as adequate food and proper conditions of working and of living. The worker must, in other words, have leisure.

SINFUL WASTE

Irregularity of employment creates hardships and demoralization of every kind. It is the most sinful waste.[16]

SKILLED AND UNSKILLED LABOR

It has been clearly demonstrated, I think, by those who have studied the possible efficiencies and economies in labor, that the distinction between skilled and unskilled is wholly

14 See also Leisure, Long Hours.
15 See Home Life.
16 See Irregularity of Employment.

unscientific and unphilosophical. There certainly is nothing that could be deemed to be nearer an unskilled occupation than lifting a pig of iron from the yard and putting it into a car; and yet it has been demonstrated by a study of that particular operation that it was possible with the same amount of exertion, or less, to produce four times the former results by knowing how to do it, by selecting the proper man to do it, by teaching him how to do it, and particularly by teaching him how to rest when he was not actually under load. Now, what is true of the loading of pig iron has been shown to be true of other occupations which are constantly called unskilled, such as the mere shoveling of coal or the mere shoveling of dirt. You could pass through the whole realm of human, manual occupation and find that the difference between the man who is skilled and the man who is unskilled is not in the occupation but is in the man and in the training of men. And in the same way the performance will be largely dependent not only upon skill but upon the physical and mental condition of the individual.

SMALL GROUPS

The great America for which we long is unattainable unless the individuality of communities becomes far more highly developed and becomes a common American phenomenon. For a century our growth has come through natural expansion and the increase of the functions of the federal government. The growth of the future—at least of the immediate future—must be in quality and spiritual value.[17] And that can come only through the concentrated, intensified strivings of smaller groups.

SMALL STOCKHOLDERS

[395] Numerous small stockholding creates in the corporation a condition of irresponsible absentee landlordism; that

---

[17] See Quality and Spiritual Value.

is, the numerous small stockholders in the steel corporation, in the tobacco company, and in the other trusts occupy a position which is dangerous to society. They have a certain degree of wealth without responsibility. Their only desire is dividends. Their demand upon the managers is at most to maintain or increase the dividends. They have no power or responsibility; they have no relations to the employees; they are remote, often thousands of miles from the people who are toiling for them. Thus we have reproduced in industry the precise conditions which brought all the misery upon Ireland and upon other countries where absentee landlordism has prevailed. Large dividends are the bribes which the managers tender the small investor for the power to use other people's money.

SOCIAL INVENTIONS

The reason why we have not made more progress in social matters is that these problems have not been tackled by the practical men of high ability, like those who have worked on industrial inventions and enterprises. We need *social inventions*, each of many able men adding his work until the invention is perfected.

SOCIALISM

The talk of the agitator alone does not advance socialism a step; but the formation of great trusts—the huge railroad consolidations—the insurance "racers" with the attendant rapacity or the dishonesty of their potent managers, and their frequent corruption of councils and legislatures is hastening us almost irresistibly into socialistic measures. The great captains of industry and of finance, who profess the greatest horror of the extension of governmental functions, are the chief makers of socialism. Socialistic thinkers smile approvingly at the operations of Morgan, Perkins and Rockefeller, and of the Hydes, McCalls and McCurdys. They see approaching the glad day when monopoly shall have brought all industry and finance under a single head, so that with the cutting of a single neck, as Nero vainly wished for his Christian subjects, destruction of the enemy may be accomplished. Our great trust-building, trust-abusing capitalists have in their selfish shortsightedness become the makers of socialism, proclaiming by their acts, like the nobles of France, "After us, The Deluge!" [18]

*

Do not believe that you can find a universal remedy for evil conditions or immoral practices in effecting a fundamental change in society (as by State Socialism).[19]

SOCIAL PROBLEMS AND SCIENTIFIC INVENTIONS

When men begin to think as hard, as intensely, about their social problems as they have thought about automobiles, aeroplanes, and wireless telegraphy, nothing will be socially impossible. Many things which have seemed inevitable will be seen to have been quite unnecessary.

SOLVING THE JEWISH PROBLEM

[400] The Jews are a people of thinkers; and they have a passion for freedom. If we acquiesce in decisions made for us and not by us, it can only be because we are practically indifferent; because we do not care, or at all events, do not care enough to assert our views, we certainly shall not care enough to make the sacrifices necessarily involved in saving our brethren, and solving the problem of the Jewish people.

SOUNDNESS OF JUDGMENT

Soundness of judgment is easily obscured by self-interest.

---

[18] See also Monopoly, Remedial Institutions.
[19] See Remedial Institutions.

SPECIALIZATION

The more complex life becomes the more we shall have to depend on the specialist. The day when any one human being could claim to be master of all knowledge is long past. Any field of learning is by now probably coextensive with that of all the humanities together of two or three hundred years ago. Today Dr. Einstein presumably knows as little about law as does Professor Roscoe Pound about nuclear physics. But since, in order to solve our problems, we must understand both the nature of law and the universe, the Einsteins and the Pounds must understand each other. But how is that to be accomplished? I believe there is only one way of doing it, and that is, postponing the age at which a student is permitted to begin working seriously on his own specialty. I would require of everyone who wished to pursue any one of the professions, arts, or sciences, an eight year college course, which would familiarize him with the major outlines of civilization, so that the specialties not his own might not be altogether alien to him. The span of life is increasing, and an additional four years of preparation should not be regarded as too great a sacrifice.

STRIKES

Labor cannot on any terms surrender the right to strike. In last resort, it is its sole effective means of protest. The old common law, which assures the employer the right to discharge and the employee the right to quit work, for any reason or for no reason in either case, is a necessary guaranty of industrial liberty.[20]

STRUGGLE

Struggle . . . is a law of life. Must we not fight, all of us, even for the peace that we most crave?

---

[20] See also Unions.

SUCCESS BUILT ON FAILURE

[405]   We are prone to think of America as the home of good investments. But nobody who has looked into American industrial and financial development can fail to know that, with the exception perhaps of the automobile and a few other recent industries, there has been hardly a single field of great business success in the United States, which does not rest on a foundation of failures. Almost every enterprise in the United States, with the exception of the Great Northern, is built upon a failure. The Atchison, Topeka, Santa Fe, and the Northern Pacific are outstanding instances of successful American railroads. But despite the rich land grants made by the government, both the Atchison and the Northern Pacific went through two receiverships. Stockholders and bondholders who lacked faith to pay burdensome assessments, or were unable to do so, lost all or much of what they personally had invested. This is true also of the original investors in the heavily subsidized Union Pacific. Most of America's 250,000 miles of railroad have a similar history. But they were great factors in our prosperity. When we think now of American successes, we think not of our beginnings but of the flowers in full bloom.

SUPPLY AND DEMAND

Of course, there isn't any such thing as a law of supply and demand as an inexorable rule. It is an economic tendency, a highly important one, and one of the most important of the economic forces; but all the time we see that there are conditions under which the law of supply and demand does not work.

TEACHERS

Teachers are largely a meek, downtrodden, unappreciated body of men. To know that others believe in them, consider them capable of high thinking and doing, and are willing to help them out—may enable them to accomplish more than even they think possible.

TESTING A FACT

No statement of facts, however honest your people may be, can be relied upon until it has been subjected to the careful study and criticism of people who have a different point of view.

THINKING

Thinking is not a heaven-born thing . . . intelligence is not a gift that merely comes. It is a gift men make and women make for themselves. It is earned, and it is earned by effort. There is no effort, to my mind, that is comparable in its qualities, that is so taxing to the individual, as to think, to analyze fundamentally.[21]

*

[410]   To think hard and persistently is painful.[22]

TRANSPORTATION

Transportation is one of the privileges which places the greatest restraint in favor of a few upon a large number of the American business men. It has been said sometimes that you cannot follow up any industrial monopoly today without finding that some unjust and preferential transportation privilege accounts in large measure for the power possessed. . . .

Privilege, preference, discrimination in favor of very large and powerful interests in the transportation field have been the main causes of the overweening growth of a few concerns as compared with the more struggling growth of many others.

---

[21] See Industrial Democracy and Thinking.
[22] See Human Nature.

TRIAL AND ERROR

The discoveries in physical science, the triumphs of invention, attest the value of the process of trial and error.[23]

TRIVIALITY

Triviality destroys at once robustness of thought and delicacy of feeling. No enthusiasm can flourish, no generous impulse can survive under its blighting influence.[24]

TRUSTEE OF HISTORY

It is not wealth, it is not station, it is not social standing and ambition, which can make us worthy of the Jewish name, of the Jewish heritage. To be worthy of them, we must live up to and with them. We must regard ourselves as their custodians. Every young man here must feel that he is the trustee of what is best in Jewish history.[25]

UNCHARTED SEAS

[415] The economic and social sciences are largely uncharted seas.[26]

UNEMPLOYMENT

Unemployment—perhaps the gravest and most difficult problem of modern industry.

*

Unemployment is as unnecessary as disease epidemics. One who says in this intelligent age that unemployment is necessary or unavoidable is like one a generation ago who would have continued to insist that epidemics were, if not necessary and divinely imposed, at least inevitable.

---

[23] See Experimentation.
[24] See Blighting Influence of Journalistic Gossip.
[25] See Jewish Heritage.
[26] See Experimentation.

UNIONISM

The essence of unionism is collective bargaining; that is, instead of the employer dealing individually with each employee, he deals with a large body through their representatives, in respect to the rate of wages and the hours and conditions of employment.

UNION LEADERS

Abuses of the trade unions have been innumerable. Individuals of slight education, of slight training, are elevated many times by shallow popularity to positions which can be filled adequately only by men possessing great minds and great characters. No wonder, then, that these leaders make mistakes; make grievous errors. The extraordinary thing is that they have not made more mistakes. It is one of the most promising symptoms in American democracy that with all the difficulties attending such positions the labor leaders on the whole have done so little that is wrong.

UNIONS [27]

[420] The employer needs the unions "to stay him from the fall of vanity"; the employees need them for their own protection; the community needs them to raise the level of the citizen.

*

The [Unions] have been largely instrumental in securing reasonable hours of labor and proper conditions of work; in raising materially the scale of wages, and in protecting women and children from industrial oppression.

The trade unions have done this, not for the workingmen alone, but for all of us; since the conditions under which so large a part of our fellow citizens work and live will deter-

---

[27] See also Employer and Employee, Employers and Unions, Strikes, Unrest.

mine, in great measure, the future of our country for good or for evil.

*

One reason why the trades union had to come into existence was because the law of supply and demand did not work properly between the opposing forces of the powerful employer and the individual worker.

*

Strong, responsible unions are essential to industrial fair play. Without them the labor bargain is wholly one-sided. The parties to the labor contract must be nearly equal in strength if justice is to be worked out, and this means that the workers must be organized and that their organizations must be recognized by employers as a condition precedent to industrial peace.

*

Nearly every American who is not himself financially interested in a particular controversy sympathizes thoroughly with every struggle of the workingmen to better their own condition. But this sympathy for the workingmen is quickly forfeited whenever the conduct of the strikers is unreasonable, arbitrary, lawless or unjust. The American people with their common sense, their desire for fair play and their respect for law, resent such conduct. The growth and success of labor unions, therefore, as well as their usefulness to the community at large, would be much advanced by any measures which tend to make them more deliberate, less arbitrary, and more patient with the trammels of a civilized community.[28]

*

[425]   A bad act is no worse, as it is no better, because it has been done by a labor union and not by a partnership or a

---

[28] See also Strikes.

business corporation. If unions are lawless, restrain and punish their lawlessness; if they are arbitrary, repress their arbitrariness; if their demands are unreasonable or unjust, resist them; but do not oppose unions as such.

*

Nearly every large strike is attended by acts of flagrant lawlessness. The employers, and a large part of the public, charge these acts to the unions. In very many instances the unions are entirely innocent. Hoodlums, or habitual criminals, have merely availed themselves of a convenient opportunity for breaking the law, in some instances even incited thereto by employers desiring to turn public opinion against the strikers. What an immense gain would come to the unions from a full and fair trial of such charges if the innocence of the unions were established, and perhaps even the guilt of an employer! And such a trial would almost necessarily be had before a jury, upon oral testimony, with full opportunity of cross-examination; whereas now, nearly every important adjudication involving the alleged action of unions is made upon application to a judge sitting alone, and upon written affidavits, without the opportunity of cross-examination.[29]

UNITED STATES STEEL CORPORATION

While this corporation is the greatest example of combination, the most conspicuous instance of combination of capital in the world, it has, as an incident of the power which it acquires through that combination and through its associations with railroads and the financial world, undertaken, and undertaken successfully, to deny the right of combination to the workingmen, and these horrible conditions of labor, which are a disgrace to America, considering the wealth which has surrounded and flown out of the in-

---

[29] See also Laws not Men, Strikes.

dustry, are the result of having killed or eliminated from the steel industry unionism. All the power of capital and all the ability and intelligence of the men who wield and who serve the capital have been used to make practically slaves of these operatives, because it does not mean merely in respect to the way in which they have lived, but the very worst part of all this is the repression. It is a condition of repression, of slavery in the real sense of the word, which is alien to American conditions.[30]

*

It is a life so inhuman as to make our former Negro slavery infinitely preferable, for the master owned the slave, and tried to keep his property in working order for his own interest. The Steel Trust, on the other hand, looks on its slaves as something to be worked out and thrown aside. The result is physical and moral degeneracy—work, work, work, without recreation or any possibility of relief save that which dissipation brings. The men coming out of these steel mills move on pay day straight to the barroom. Think what such men transmit as a physical and moral heritage to their children and think of our American citizenship for men who live under such conditions.

There is only one explanation. This great corporation, which exemplifies the power of combination, and in connection with which combination has been justified, has made it its first business to prevent combination among its employees when they sought to procure decent working conditions and living conditions. It stamped out, through its immense powers of endurance, one strike after another. It developed a secret service, a system of espionage among its workmen, singling out individuals who favor unionism; and anyone fomenting dissatisfaction with existing conditions, as it was called, was quietly discharged. The trust is but-

---

[30] Thanks to the work of Mr. Brandeis, conditions in the steel industry are considerably different from what they were in 1912.

tressed on one hand by the powers of the railroads and on the other by great financial interests; against it stands the poor miserable individual workingman.

UNITED STATES SUPREME COURT

There is no reason why five gentlemen of the Supreme Court should know better what public policy demands than five gentlemen of Congress. In the absence of legislation by Congress the Supreme Court expresses its idea of public policy, but in the last analysis it is the function of the legislative branch of the government to declare the public policy of the United States. There are a great many rules which the Supreme Court lays down which may afterwards be changed, and are afterwards changed, by legislation. It is not disrespect to the Supreme Court to do it. Their interpretation of the law may be set aside by a new law.

*

[430]   If the Court is of opinion that this act of Congress is in necessary conflict with its recent decisions, those cases should be frankly overruled. The reasons for doing so are persuasive. Our experience in attempting to apply the rule, and helpful discussions by friends of the Court, have made it clear that the rule declared is legally unsound; that it disturbs legal principles long established; and that if adhered to, it will make a serious addition to the classes of cases which this Court is required to review. Experience and discussion have also made apparent how unfortunate are the results, economically and socially. It has, in part, frustrated a promising attempt to alleviate some of the misery, and remove some of the injustice, incident to the conduct of industry and commerce. These far-reaching and unfortunate results of the rule declared in *Southern Pacific Co. v. Jensen* cannot have been foreseen when the decision was rendered. If it is adhered to, appropriate legislative provision, urgently needed, cannot be made until another amendment of the

Constitution shall have been adopted. For no federal workmen's compensation law could satisfy the varying and peculiar economic and social needs incident to the diversity
of conditions in the several States.

*

This Court cannot issue declaratory decrees.

*

It is not our province to weigh evidence. Put at its highest, our function is to determine, in the light of all facts
which may enrich our knowledge and enlarge our understanding, whether the measure, enacted in the exercise of
an unquestioned police power and of a character inherently unobjectionable, transcends the bounds of reason;
that is, whether the provision as applied is so clearly arbitrary or capricious that legislators acting reasonably could
not have believed it to be necessary or appropriate for the
public welfare.

*

It is a peculiar virtue of our system of law that the process
of inclusion and exclusion, so often employed in developing
a rule, is not allowed to end with its enunciation and that an
expression in an opinion yields later to the impact of facts
unforeseen. The attitude of the Court in this respect has
been especially helpful when called upon to adjust the re-
spective powers of the States and the Nation in the field
of taxation.[31]

UNITY

Absence of discord does not imply unity. Absence of discord may be due to indifference. Unity implies interest and
participation. There may be acquiescence in the decision of
a self-constituted body purporting to act on behalf of a free
people. But there cannot be unity of action of a free people

---

[31] See also Experimentation.

unless the decision is the act of that people participating through its properly constituted representatives.

UNIVERSITY

[435]   Money alone cannot build a worthy University. Too much money—or too quick money—may mar one; particularly if it is foreign money. To become great, a University must express the people whom it serves, and must express the people and the community at their best. The aim must be high and the vision broad; the goal seemingly attainable but beyond the immediate reach.

*

The function of the University in respect to the fine arts is not limited to promoting understanding and appreciation. It should strive to awaken the slumbering creative instinct, to encourage its exercise and development, to stimulate production.

UNREST [32]

The real cause that is disturbing business today is not the uncertainty as to the interpretation of "reasonable" or "unreasonable" restraint of trade; it is this social unrest of our people in this struggle with which none in our history save the Revolution and the Civil War can be compared.

*

The only way to meet the socialistic and restless spirit of the times is to meet and remove each individual case of injustice.

*

My observation leads me to believe that while there are many contributing causes to unrest, that there is one cause which is fundamental. That is, necessary conflict—the con-

---

[32] See also Industrial Absolutism.

trast between our political liberty and our industrial absolutism.[33]

*

[440] Unrest means ordinarily unused faculties, and there will be labor unrest until the faculties of the laboring man are fully utilized, and they cannot be without a share in the responsibility for the results of the business in which they are engaged.[34]

*

Unrest will be to a certain extent mitigated by anything which improves the condition of the workers, and I cannot see any real solution, ultimate solution, or an approximation of a solution of unrest as long as there exists in this country any juxtaposition of political democracy and industrial absolutism. To my mind, before we can really solve the problem of industrial unrest, the worker must have a part in the responsibility and management of the business, and whether we adopt scientific management, or adopt any other form of obtaining compensation or of increasing productivity, unrest will not be removed as long as we have that inconsistency, as I view it.

UNRESTRICTED POWER

I should not rely upon the goodness of heart of anybody. Neither our character nor our intelligence can long bear the strain of unrestricted power.

*

The sense of unrestricted power is just as demoralizing for the employer as it is for the employee.[35]

---

[33] See Monopoly.
[34] See also Unions.
[35] See also Employer and Employee.

UNWIELDY COMMITTEES

Unwieldy committees were devised by autocrats whose advantage it is to pose as being democrats.

VALUE

[445]   Value is a word of many meanings.

VITAL AND BEYOND PRICE

But precisely because I believe in this future in which material comfort is to be comparatively easy of attainment, I also believe that the race must steadily insist upon preserving its moral vigor unweakened. It is not good for us that we should ever lose the fighting quality, the stamina, and the courage to battle for what we want when we are convinced that we are entitled to it, and other means fail. There is something better than peace, and that is the peace that is won by struggle.[36] We shall have lost something vital and beyond price on the day when the State denies us the right to resort to force in defense of a just cause.

WAR

The cause of a war—as of most human action—is not single. War is ordinarily the result of many cooperating causes, many different conditions, acts, and motives. Historians rarely agree in their judgment as to what was the determining factor in a particular war, even when they write under circumstances where detachment and the availability of evidence from all sources minimize both prejudice and other sources of error; for individuals, and classes of individuals, attach significance to those things which are significant to them. And, as the contributing causes cannot be subjected, like a chemical combination in a test tube, to qualitative and quantitative analysis so as to weigh and value the various elements, the historians differ necessarily

---

[36] See Better Than Peace.

in their judgments. One finds the determining cause of war in a great man; another in an idea, a belief, an economic necessity, a trade advantage, a sinister machination, or an accident. It is for this reason largely that men seek to interpret anew in each age, and often with each generation, the important events in the world's history.

WAR AND ITS AFTERMATH

Europe was devastated by war, we by the aftermath.

WHITE PAPER ON PALESTINE

The White Paper does no credit to the moral integrity of British statesmen. Nor even to their diplomatic skill.[37]

WIRE TAPPING[38]

[450] The progress of science in furnishing the Government with means of espionage is not likely to stop with wire tapping. Ways may some day be developed by which the Government, without removing papers from secret drawers, can reproduce them in court, and by which it will be enabled to expose to a jury the most intimate occurrences of the home. Advances in the psychic and related sciences may bring means of exploring unexpressed beliefs, thoughts, and emotions. "That places the liberty of every man in the hands of every petty officer" was said by James Otis of much lesser intrusions than these. To Lord Camden a far slighter intrusion seemed "subversive of all the comforts of society." Can it be that the Constitution affords no protection against such invasions of individual security?

[37] Justice Brandeis was referring to the British White Paper on Palestine of 1939.
[38] See also Government Intrusion.

WOMEN

Women often have greater opportunities than men to bring about social reform, for which all of us are working. They have the desire, enthusiasm and understanding.

WOMEN—OVERWORK

The experience of manufacturing countries has illustrated the evil effect of overwork upon the general welfare. Deterioration of any large proportion of the population inevitably lowers the entire community physically, mentally, and morally. When the health of women has been injured by long hours, not only is the working efficiency of the community impaired, but the deterioration is handed down to succeeding generations. Infant mortality rises, while the children of married workingwomen who survive are injured by inevitable neglect. The overwork of future mothers thus directly attacks the welfare of the nation.

ZIONISM [39]

It [Zionism] is not a movement to remove all the Jews of the world compulsorily to Palestine. In the first place there are 14,000,000 Jews, and Palestine would not accommodate more than one-third of that number. In the second place, it is not a movement to compel anyone to go to Palestine. It is essentially a movement to give to the Jew more, not less freedom; it aims to enable the Jews to exercise the same right now exercised by practically every other people in the world: To live at their option either in the land of their fathers or in some other country; a right which members of small nations as well as of large, which Irish, Greek, Bulgarian, Serbian, or Belgian, may now exercise as fully as Germans or English.

Zionism seeks to establish in Palestine, for such Jews as

[39] See also Noblesse Oblige.

choose to go and remain there, and for their descendants, a legally secured home, where they may live together and lead a Jewish life, where they may expect ultimately to constitute a majority of the population, and may look forward to what we should call home rule. The Zionists seek to establish this home in Palestine because they are convinced that the undying longing of Jews for Palestine is a fact of deepest significance; that it is a manifestation in the struggle for existence by an ancient people which has established its right to live, a people whose three thousand years of civilization has produced a faith, culture and individuality which will enable it to contribute largely in the future, as it has in the past, to the advance of civilization; and that it is not a right merely but a duty of the Jewish nationality to survive and develop. They believe that only in Palestine can Jewish life be fully protected from the forces of disintegration; that there alone can the Jewish spirit reach its full and natural development; and that by securing for those Jews who wish to settle there the opportunity to do so, not only those Jews, but all other Jews will be benefited, and that the long perplexing Jewish Problem will, at last, find solution.

*

Zionism suffers from a superfluity of orators and a dearth of statesmen.

ZIONISM AND PATRIOTISM

[455]   Let no American imagine that Zionism is inconsistent with Patriotism. Multiple loyalties are objectionable only if they are inconsistent. A man is a better citizen of the United States for being also a loyal citizen of his state, and of his city; for being loyal to his family, and to his profession or trade; for being loyal to his college or his lodge. Every Irish American who contributed towards advancing home rule was a better man and a better American for the sacrifice he

made. Every American Jew who aids in advancing the Jewish settlement in Palestine, though he feels that neither he nor his descendants will ever live there, will likewise be a better man and a better American for doing so.

*

BIOGRAPHICAL NOTES

The numbers to the left of the notes refer back to the passages in the text. In the latter, to keep the margin of the page clear, only each fifth passage is marked. The reader should not find it difficult to fit together the in-between passages with their proper numbers. Since this little book is not intended for the scholar, the references are as a rule given to the books by and on Justice Brandeis that are conveniently available, and not to the Journals, Magazines, Law Reviews, or Reports in which they first appeared. Those interested in tracing a quotation to its original source will be able to do so, generally, by looking up the reference here given. Thus, for example, the quotations from Ernest Poole are referred back to *Business—A Profession*. There the reader will learn that Mr. Poole's essay was first published in the *American Magazine*, February, 1911.

1 Mason, *A Free Man's Life,* p. 505.

2 *Idem, The Brandeis Way,* p. 71.

3 *Idem, Brandeis and the Modern State,* pp. 79 f.

4 In a conversation with me.

5 In a conversation with me.

6 Lief, *Social and Economic Views of Mr. Justice Brandeis,* p. 15.

7 Ernest Poole, Foreword to *Business—A Profession,* p. liv.

8 In a conversation with me.

9 Brandeis, *Business—A Profession,* pp. 372 f.

10 Mason, *A Free Man's Life,* p. 531.

11 Brandeis, *Letter to Frederick Wehle,* October 28, 1924. In Flexner, *Mr. Justice Brandeis and the University of Louisville,* p. 24.

12 *Idem, Other People's Money,* p. 50.

13 Fraenkel, *The Curse of Bigness,* p. 35.

14 Brandeis, *Business—A Profession,* p. 58.

15 *Idem, Ibid.,* pp. 366 f.

16 Fraenkel, *The Curse of Bigness,* p. 81.

17 *Idem, Ibid.,* p. 73.

18 *Idem, Ibid.,* p. 51.

19 Brandeis, *Business—A Profession,* pp. 365 f.

20 In a conversation with me.

21 Brandeis, *Letter to Alfred Brandeis,* January 16, 1927. In Flexner, *Mr. Justice Brandeis and the University of Louisville,* p. 53.

22 *Idem, Business—A Profession,* p. 367.

23 Goldman, *Brandeis on Zionism,* p. 29.

24 *Idem, Ibid.*

25 In a conversation with me.

26 In a conversation with me.

27 Fraenkel, *The Curse of Bigness,* pp. 44 f.

28 Lief, *Social and Economic Views of Mr. Justice Brandeis,* p. 261.

29 Mason, *A Free Man's Life,* p. 200.

30 Lief, *Social and Economic Views of Mr. Justice Brandeis,* p. 141.

31 Brandeis, *Letter to Fanny Brandeis,* October 20, 1924. In Flexner, *Mr. Justice Brandeis and the University of Louisville,* p. 16.

32 Lief, *Social and Economic Views of Mr. Justice Brandeis,* p. 153.

33 Fraenkel, *The Curse of Bigness,* p. 40.

34 *Idem, Ibid.,* p. 41.

35 Brandeis, *Other People's Money*, p. 109.

36 *Idem, Ibid.*, pp. 44 f.

37 *Idem, Ibid.*, pp. 201 f.

38 *Idem, Ibid.*, pp. 198 ff.

39 *Idem, Ibid.*, pp. 22 f.

40 Fraenkel, *The Curse of Bigness*, p. 263.

41 *Idem, Ibid.*, p. 46.

42 In a conversation with me.

43 Brandeis, *Business—A Profession*, p. 12.

44 Lief, *Brandeis: The Personal History of an American Ideal*, pp. 220 f.

45 Brandeis, *Other People's Money*, p. 163.

46 *Idem, Business—A Profession*, p. 287.

47 Mason, *Brandeis and the Modern State*, p. 58.

48 Frankfurter, *Mr. Justice Brandeis*, p. 133.

49 Fraenkel, *The Curse of Bigness*, p. 107.

50 *Idem, Ibid.*, p. 292.

51 *Idem, Ibid.*, p. 160.

52 *Idem, Ibid.*, p. 36.

53 Brandeis, *Business—A Profession*, pp. 370 f.

54 *Idem, Ibid.*, p. 89.

55 *Idem, Ibid.*, p. 1.

56 Fraenkel, *The Curse of Bigness*, pp. 141 f.

57 Brandeis, *Business—A Profession*, pp. 4 f.

58 Lief, *Social and Economic Views of Mr. Justice Brandeis*, p. 212.

59 Fraenkel, *The Curse of Bigness*, p. 185.

60 Brandeis, *Letter to Alfred Brandeis*, February 18, 1925. In Flexner, *Mr. Justice Brandeis and the University of Louisville*, p. 8.

61 *Idem, Business—A Profession*, pp. 346 ff.

62 Lief, *Social and Economic Views of Mr. Justice Brandeis*, p. 410.

63 Mason, *A Free Man's Life*, p. 94.

64 Goldman, *Brandeis on Zionism*, p. 64.

65 Brandeis, *Business—A Profession*, p. 370.

66 In a conversation with me.

67 Fraenkel, *The Curse of Bigness*, pp. 270 f.

68 In a conversation with me.

69 Brandeis, *Business—A Profession*, pp. 348 f.

70 Fraenkel, *The Curse of Bigness*, pp. 78 f.

71 Mason, *Brandeis and the Modern State*, p. 67.

72 Ernest Poole, Foreword to *Business—A Profession*, pp. xlv f.

73 Fraenkel, *The Curse of Bigness*, p. 105.

74 Lief, *Social and Economic Views of Mr. Justice Brandeis*, p. 80.

75 *Idem, Ibid.*, pp. 398 f.

76 *Idem, Brandeis: The Personal History of an American Ideal*, p. 450.

77 *Idem, Ibid.*, p. 123.

78 Fraenkel, *The Curse of Bigness*, p. 197.

79 *Idem, Ibid.*, pp. 106 f.

80 *Idem, Ibid.*, p. 76.

81 Ernest Poole, Foreword to *Business—A Profession*, p. xii.

82 Lief, *Social and Economic Views of Mr. Justice Brandeis*, p. 390.

83 Mason, *The Brandeis Way*, p. 166.

84 Fraenkel, *The Curse of Bigness*, p. 69.

85 Brandeis, *Business—A Profession*, pp. 368 f.

86 *Idem, Other People's Money*, pp. 222 f.

87 *Idem, Business—A Profession*, p. 337.

88 Ernest Poole, Foreword to *Business—A Profession*, p. lv.

89 Lief, *Social and Economic Views of Mr. Justice Brandeis*, p. 399.

90 Mason, *Brandeis and the Modern State*, p. 79.

91 Brandeis, *Business—A Profession*, p. 125.

92 *Idem, Other People's Money*, p. 204.

93 Fraenkel, *The Curse of Bigness*, p. 88.

94 Brandeis, *Letter to Stella and Emily Dembitz*, May 17, 1926. In Flexner, *Mr. Justice Brandeis and the University of Louisville*, pp. 36 f.

95 Goldman, *Brandeis on Zionism*, p. 91.

96 Mason, *Brandeis and the Modern State*, p. 102.

97 *Idem, A Free Man's Life*, p. 382.

98 Brandeis, *Business—A Profession*, p. 371.

99 Goldman, *Brandeis on Zionism*, p. 64.

100 *Idem, Ibid.*

101 Brandeis, *Business—A Profession*, p. 29.

102 Mason, *A Free Man's Life*, p. 520.

103 Lief, *Social and Economic Views of Mr. Justice Brandeis*, p. 196.

104 Brandeis, *Business—A Profession*, p. 278.

105 *Idem, Other People's Money*, p. 44.

106 Idem, Business—A Profession, p. 372.

107 In a conversation with me.

108 Lief, Brandeis: The Personal History of an American Ideal, p. 277.

109 Goldman, Brandeis on Zionism, p. 64.

110 Lief, Social and Economic Views of Mr. Justice Brandeis, p. 26.

111 Goldman, Brandeis on Zionism, p. 64.

112 Idem, Ibid., p. 67.

113 Brandeis, Business—A Profession, p. 368.

114 Fraenkel, The Curse of Bigness, p. 82.

115 Brandeis, Business—A Profession, p. 32.

116 Mason, A Free Man's Life, p. 602.

117 Lief, Social and Economic Views of Mr. Justice Brandeis, p. 165.

118 Brandeis, Business—A Profession, p. 3.

119 Idem, Ibid., pp. 206 f.

120 Idem, Other People's Money, pp. 204 f.

121 Fraenkel, The Curse of Bigness, p. 51.

122 Brandeis, Other People's Money, p. 202.

123 Fraenkel, The Curse of Bigness, pp. 85 f.

124 Mason, A Free Man's Life, p. 38.

125 Idem, Ibid., p. 141.

126 Fraenkel, The Curse of Bigness, pp. 92 f.

127 Brandeis, Business—A Profession, p. 17.

128 Idem, Ibid., pp. 21 f.

129 Fraenkel, The Curse of Bigness, pp. 85 f.

130 Idem, Ibid., pp. 89 f.

131 Idem, Ibid., p. 95.

132 Mason, A Free Man's Life, p. 529.

133 Fraenkel, The Curse of Bigness, p. 87.

134 Brandeis, Business—A Profession, pp. 364 f.

135 Mason, Brandeis and the Modern State, pp. 95 f.

136 Fraenkel, The Curse of Bigness, p. 114.

137 Lief, Brandeis: The Personal History of an American Ideal, p. 78.

138 Brandeis, Business—A Profession, pp. 338 f.

139 Fraenkel, The Curse of Bigness, p. 270.

140 Idem, Ibid., pp. 156 ff.

141 Idem, Ibid., pp. 68 f.

142 Lief, Social and Economic Views of Mr. Justice Brandeis, p. 5.

143 Idem, Ibid., p. 411.

144 Ernest Poole, Foreword to *Business—A Profession*, pp. liv f.

145 Fraenkel, *The Curse of Bigness*, p. 24.

146 Brandeis, *Business—A Profession*, pp. 127 f.

147 Lief, *Social and Economic Views of Mr. Justice Brandeis*, p. 261.

148 Brandeis, *Business—A Profession*, pp. 58 f.

149 Ernest Poole, Foreword to *Business—A Profession*, pp. lii f.

150 Brandeis, *Business—A Profession*, p. 369.

151 Lief, *Social and Economic Views of Mr. Justice Brandeis*, pp. 260 ff.

152 *Idem, Ibid.*, pp. 212 ff.

153 *Idem, Ibid.*, p. 236.

154 *Idem, Ibid.*, pp. 235 f.

155 *Idem, Ibid.*, p. 259.

156 *Idem, Ibid.*, p. 260.

157 *Idem, Ibid.*, p. 264.

158 *Idem, Ibid.*, p. 231.

159 *Idem, Ibid.*, p. 261.

160 In a conversation with me.

161 In a conversation with me.

162 Brandeis, *Business—A Profession*, p. 3.

163 Lief, *Social and Economic Views of Mr. Justice Brandeis*, p. 284.

164 *Idem, Ibid.*, p. 271.

165 Ernest Poole, Foreword to *Business—A Profession*, p. lii.

166 Mason, *A Free Man's Life*, p. 281.

167 Lief, *Social and Economic Views of Mr. Justice Brandeis*, p. 281.

168 *Idem, Ibid.*, pp. 280 f.

169 *Idem, Ibid.*, p. 391.

170 Ernest Poole, Foreword to *Business—A Profession*, p. xxvi.

171 Brandeis, *Other People's Money*, p. 50.

172 Lief, *Social and Economic Views of Mr. Justice Brandeis*, p. 261.

173 Mason, *Brandeis and the Modern State*, p. 98.

174 *Idem, A Free Man's Life*, p. 80.

175 Lief, *Brandeis: The Personal History of an American Ideal*, p. 205.

176 Brandeis, *Business—A Profession*, p. 361.

177 Lief, *Social and Economic Views of Mr. Justice Brandeis*, p. 236.

178 Goldman, *Brandeis on Zionism*, pp. 27 f.

179 *Idem, Ibid.*, p. 52.

180 *Idem, Ibid.*, p. 100.

181 In a conversation with me.

182 Lief, *Social and Economic Views of Mr. Justice Brandeis*, p. 345.

183 Mason, *Brandeis and the Modern State*, p. 31.

184 Brandeis, *Business—A Profession*, pp. 37 f.

185 *Idem, Other People's Money*, p. 23.

186 Lief, *Brandeis: The Personal History of an American Ideal*, p. 123.

187 Fraenkel, *The Curse of Bigness*, p. 292.

188 Lief, *Social and Economic Views of Mr. Justice Brandeis*, p. 410.

189 In a conversation with me.

190 Brandeis, *Letter to Alfred Brandeis*, January 16, 1927. In Flexner, *Mr. Justice Brandeis and the University of Louisville*, p. 53.

191 Fraenkel, *The Curse of Bigness*, pp. 267 ff.

192 Goldman, *Brandeis on Zionism*, p. 98.

193 Brandeis, *Business—A Profession*, p. 342.

194 Fraenkel, *The Curse of Bigness*, pp. 73 f.

195 Ernest Poole, Foreword to *Business—A Profession*, pp. xxxviii f.

196 Brandeis, *Other People's Money*, p. 208.

197 Fraenkel, *The Curse of Bigness*, p. 79.

198 *Idem, Ibid.*, pp. 35 f.

199 Mason, *A Free Man's Life*, p. 372.

200 Brandeis, *Business—A Profession*, p. 16.

201 Fraenkel, *The Curse of Bigness*, p. 80.

202 *Idem, Ibid.*, p. 39.

203 Lief, *Social and Economic Views of Mr. Justice Brandeis*, pp. 373 f.

204 Brandeis, *Business—A Profession*, p. 27.

205 *Idem, Ibid.*, p. 26.

206 Mason, *Brandeis and the Modern State*, p. 206.

207 Ernest Poole, Foreword to *Business—A Profession*, p. xx.

208 Brandeis, *Business—A Profession*, pp. 324 f.

209 Lief, *Brandeis: The Personal History of an American Ideal*, p. 290.

210 Brandeis, *Other People's Money*, p. 51.

211 *Idem, Ibid.*, p. 99.

212 *Idem, Business—A Profession*, p. 45.

213 Fraenkel, *The Curse of Bigness*, p. 157.

214 Goldman, *Brandeis on Zionism*, pp. 14 f.

215 *Idem, Ibid.*, p. 153.

216 In a conversation with me.

217 Goldman, *Brandeis on Zionism*, p. 41.

218 *Idem, Ibid.*, pp. 22 f.

219 *Idem, Ibid.*, pp. 61 f.

220 *Idem, Ibid.*, p. 22.

221 *Idem, Ibid.*, p. 44.

222 *Idem, Ibid.*, pp. 12 f.

223 Mason, *A Free Man's Life*, p. 486.

224 Goldman, *Brandeis on Zionism*, pp. 13 f.

225 *Idem, Ibid.*, p. 29.

226 *Idem, Ibid.*, p. 42.

227 *Idem, Ibid.*, pp. 63 ff.

228 *Idem, Ibid.*, p. 36.

229 In a conversation with me.

230 Mason, *A Free Man's Life*, p. 532.

231 Ernest Poole, Foreword to *Business—A Profession*, p. liv.

232 Brandeis, *Business—A Profession*, pp. 361 f.

233 Ernest Poole, Foreword to *Business—A Profession*, pp. liv f.

234 Brandeis, *Business—A Profession*, p. 320.

235 Fraenkel, *The Curse of Bigness*, pp. 86 f.

236 Brandeis, *Business—A Profession*, p. 350.

237 Ernest Poole, Foreword to *Business—A Profession*, p. liv.

238 Lief, *Social and Economic Views of Mr. Justice Brandeis*, p. 325.

239 *Idem, Ibid.*, pp. 29 f.

240 Brandeis, *Business—A Profession*, pp. 362 f.

241 Mason, *Brandeis and the Modern State*, pp. 218 f.

242 As phrased by Professor Mason, *Idem, Ibid.*, p. 221.

243 Brandeis, *Business—A Profession*, p. 98.

244 Lief, *Social and Economic Views of Mr. Justice Brandeis*, p. 267.

245 Brandeis, *Business—A Profession*, pp. 359 ff.

246 Mason, *A Free Man's Life*, p. 80.

247 Ernest Poole, Foreword to *Business—A Profession*, p. x.

248 *Idem, Ibid.*, p. lv f.

249 Lief, *Social and Economic Views of Mr. Justice Brandeis*, p. 402.

250 Brandeis, *Business—A Profession*, pp. 331 f.

251 Ernest Poole, Foreword to *Business—A Profession*, p. lvi.

252 Brandeis, *Business—A Profession*, pp. 338 f.

253 *Idem, Ibid.*, p. 349.

254 *Idem, Ibid.*, p. 29.

255 The reference escapes me.

256 Brandeis, *Business—A Profession*, p. 368.

257 *Idem, Ibid.*, p. 34.

258 *Idem, Ibid.*, p. 29.

259 Goldman, *Brandeis on Zionism*, p. 17.

260 Brandeis, *Letter to Charles G. Tachau*, April 22, 1926. In Flexner, *Mr. Justice Brandeis and the University of Louisville*, p. 32.

261 *Idem, Business—A Profession*, p. 24.

262 Lief, *Social and Economic Views of Mr. Justice Brandeis*, p. 377.

263 *Idem, Ibid.*, p. 240.

264 Fraenkel, *The Curse of Bigness*, p. 89.

265 *Idem, Ibid.*, p. 268.

266 Brandeis, *Other People's Money*, p. 208.

267 *Idem, Business—A Profession*, p. 364.

268 Lief, *Social and Economic Views of Mr. Justice Brandeis*, p. 281.

269 Brandeis, *Business—A Profession*, p. 330.

270 *Idem, Letter to Alfred Brandeis*, January 16, 1927. In Flexner, *Mr. Justice Brandeis and the University of Louisville*, p. 13.

271 Mason, *Brandeis and the Modern State*, pp. 218 f.

272 Brandeis, *Business—A Profession*, p. 355.

273 Mason, *Brandeis and the Modern State*, p. 231.

274 Lief, *Social and Economic Views of Mr. Justice Brandeis*, p. 376.

275 Brandeis, *Business—A Profession*, p. 367.

276 Lief, *Social and Economic Views of Mr. Justice Brandeis*, p. 344.

277 *Idem, Ibid.*, p. 343.

278 Fraenkel, *The Curse of Bigness*, p. 56.

279 Lief, *Brandeis: The Personal History of an American Ideal*, p. 173.

280 Brandeis, *Business—A Profession*, p. 6.

281 Goldman, *Brandeis on Zionism*, p. 82.

282 Brandeis, *Business—A Profession*, p. 49.

283 Fraenkel, *The Curse of Bigness*, p. 270.

284 Mason, *A Free Man's Life*, p. 91.

285 Fraenkel, *The Curse of Bigness*, p. 159.

286 Brandeis, *Business—A Profession*, p. 154.

287 Mason, *A Free Man's Life*, p. 94.

288 *Idem, Ibid.*, p. 506.

289 In a conversation with me.

290 Lief, *Social and Economic Views of Mr. Justice Brandeis*, p. 378.

291 In a conversation with me.

292 Brandeis, *Letter to Alfred Brandeis*, February 18, 1925. In Flexner, *Mr. Justice Brandeis and the University of Louisville*, p. 9.

293 Fraenkel, *The Curse of Bigness*, p. 40.

294 Lief, *Social and Economic Views of Mr. Justice Brandeis*, pp. 314 f.

295 *Idem, Ibid.*, p. 228.

296 Fraenkel, *The Curse of Bigness*, pp. 165 f.

297 *Idem, Ibid.*, pp. 169 f.

298 *Idem, Ibid.*, p. 80.

299 Mason, *Brandeis and the Modern State*, pp. 88 f.

300 *Idem, Ibid.*, p. 83.

301 Fraenkel, *The Curse of Bigness*, p. 76.

302 *Idem, Ibid.*, pp. 72 f.

303 Mason, *Brandeis and the Modern State*, p. 79.

304 *Idem, A Free Man's Life*, p. 359.

305 Brandeis, *Other People's Money*, pp. 47 ff.

306 *Idem, Business—A Profession*, pp. 158 f.

307 *Idem, Ibid.*, p. 278.

308 Lief, *Social and Economic Views of Mr. Justice Brandeis*, pp. 401 f.

309 *Idem, Brandeis: The Personal History of an American Ideal*, p. 123.

310 *Idem, Ibid.*, p. 205.

311 Brandeis, *Other People's Money*, pp. 207 f.

312 *Idem, Ibid.*, p. 201.

313 Fraenkel, *The Curse of Bigness*, p. 105.

314 *Idem, Ibid.*

315 *Idem, Ibid.*, p. 91.

316 Goldman, *Brandeis on Zionism*, pp. 10 f.

317 *Idem, Ibid.*, pp. 17 f.

318 *Idem, Ibid.*, pp. 19 f.

319 Lief, *Social and Economic Views of Mr. Justice Brandeis*, p. 29.

320 In a conversation with me.

321 Lief, *Social and Economic Views of Mr. Justice Brandeis*, pp. 68 f.

322 Brandeis, *Other People's Money*, p. 51.

323 Mason, *Brandeis and the Modern State*, pp. 95 f.

324 Goldman, *Brandeis on Zionism*, p. 30.

325 Ernest Poole, Foreword to *Business—A Profession*, p. li.

326 Brandeis, *Other People's Money*, p. 208.

327 Fraenkel, *The Curse of Bigness*, p. 110.

328 Brandeis, *Business—A Profession*, pp. 223 f.

329 *Idem, Ibid.*, p. 276.

330 *Idem, Ibid.*, p. 71.

331 Goldman, *Brandeis on Zionism*, p. 127.

332 Mason, *A Free Man's Life*, p. 544.

333 *Idem, Ibid.*, p. 27.

334 Goldman, *Brandeis on Zionism*, p. 93.

335 Lief, *Social and Economic Views of Mr. Justice Brandeis*, p. 128.

336 Brandeis, *Business—A Profession*, p. 61.

337 Fraenkel, *The Curse of Bigness*, p. 40.

338 Mason, *Brandeis and the Modern State*, p. 97.

339 Brandeis, *Other People's Money*, pp. 17 ff.

340 Fraenkel, *The Curse of Bigness*, p. 265.

341 *Idem, Ibid.*, p. 41.

342 *Idem, Ibid.*, p. 45.

343 In a conversation with me.

344 Mason, *A Free Man's Life*, p. 519.

345 Lief, *Social and Economic Views of Mr. Justice Brandeis*, p. 399.

346 *Idem, Brandeis: The Personal History of an American Ideal*, p. 72.

347 Fraenkel, *The Curse of Bigness*, p. 86.

348 Lief, *Social and Economic Views of Mr. Justice Brandeis*, pp. 59 f.

349 *Idem, Ibid.*, pp. 372 f.

350 Brandeis, *Business—A Profession*, p. 278.

351 *Idem, Ibid.*, pp. 21 f.

352 Ernest Poole, Foreword to *Business—A Profession*, p. liii.

353 *Idem, Ibid.*, p. liv.

354 Fraenkel, *The Curse of Bigness*, p. 311.

355 Mason, *A Free Man's Life*, p. 125.

356 Brandeis, *Other People's Money*, p. 92.

357 Fraenkel, *The Curse of Bigness*, p. 264.

358 *Idem, Ibid.*, p. 266.

359 In a conversation with me.

360 Goldman, *Brandeis on Zionism*, p. 64.

361 Mason, *A Free Man's Life*, p. 603.

362 In a conversation with me.

363 Frankfurter, *Mr. Justice Brandeis*, p. 78.

364 Mason, *A Free Man's Life*, p. 38.

365 Fraenkel, *The Curse of Bigness*, pp. 104, 113 f.

366 Lief, *Social and Economic Views of Mr. Justice Brandeis*, p. 388.

367 Fraenkel, *The Curse of Bigness*, p. 270.

368 Brandeis, *Letter to Dean Warwick Anderson*, June 4, 1926. In Flexner, *Mr. Justice Brandeis and the University of Louisville*, p. 38.

369 Fraenkel, *The Curse of Bigness*, p. 270.

370 In a conversation with me.

371 In a conversation with me.

372 As phrased by Professor Mason, *Brandeis and the Modern State*, p. 236.

373 Fraenkel, *The Curse of Bigness*, p. 315.

374 Goldman, *Brandeis on Zionism*, p. 153.

375 In a conversation with me.

376 Frankfurter, *Mr. Justice Brandeis*, p. 105.

377 In a conversation with me.

378 Mason, *A Free Man's Life*, p. 164.

379 Fraenkel, *The Curse of Bigness*, p. 48.

380 *Idem, Ibid.*, p. 49.

381 Ernest Poole, Foreword to *Business—A Profession*, pp. xlviii f.

382 In a conversation with me.

383 Brandeis, *Other People's Money*, p. 103.

384 *Idem, Ibid.*, p. 6.

385 *Idem, Business—A Profession*, p. 21.

386 Lief, *Brandeis: The Personal History of an American Ideal*, p. 280.

387 Fraenkel, *The Curse of Bigness*, pp. 126 f.

388 Brandeis, *Business—A Profession*, p. 23.

389 Lief, *Social and Economic Views of Mr. Justice Brandeis*, p. 345.

390 *Idem, Ibid.*, p. 346.

391 Brandeis, *Business—A Profession*, p. 368.

392 *Idem, Ibid.*, p. 45.

393 Lief, *Social and Economic Views of Mr. Justice Brandeis*, p. 379.

394 Mason, *A Free Man's Life*, p. 603.

395 Lief, *Social and Economic Views of Mr. Justice Brandeis*, p. 375.

396 Ernest Poole, Foreword to *Business—A Profession*, p. lii.

397 Brandeis, *Business—A Profession*, pp. 158 f.

398 Fraenkel, *The Curse of Bigness*, p. 270.

399 *Idem, Ibid.*, p. 40.

400 Goldman, *Brandeis on Zionism*, p. 103.

401 Brandeis, *Other People's Money*, p. 198.

402 In a conversation with me.

403 Fraenkel, *The Curse of Bigness*, pp. 43 f.

404 *Idem, Ibid.*, p. 45.

405 Goldman, *Brandeis on Zionism*, pp. 130 f.

406 Lief, *Social and Economic Views of Mr. Justice Brandeis*, p. 378.

407 Brandeis, *Letter to Frederick Wehle*, November 19, 1924. In Flexner, *Mr. Justice Brandeis and the University of Louisville*, p. 5.

408 Lief, *Social and Economic Views of Mr. Justice Brandeis*, p. 411.

409 Fraenkel, *The Curse of Bigness*, p. 36.

410 Brandeis, *Business—A Profession*, p. 38.

411 Fraenkel, *The Curse of Bigness*, p. 138.

412 *Idem, Ibid.*, p. 159.

413 *Idem, Ibid.*, p. 292.

414 Goldman, *Brandeis on Zionism*, p. 41.

415 Fraenkel, *The Curse of Bigness*, p. 158.

416 Lief, *Social and Economic Views of Mr. Justice Brandeis*, p. 10.

417 Fraenkel, *The Curse of Bigness*, p. 41.

418 Brandeis, *Business—A Profession*, p. 46.

419 Lief, *Social and Economic Views of Mr. Justice Brandeis*, p. 374.

420 Brandeis, *Business—A Profession*, p. 19.

421 *Idem, Ibid.*, p. 88.

422 Lief, *Social and Economic Views of Mr. Justice Brandeis*, p. 378.

423 Fraenkel, *The Curse of Bigness*, p. 43.

424 Brandeis, *Business—A Profession*, pp. 91 f.

425 Mason, *A Free Man's Life*, p. 142.

426 Brandeis, *Business—A Profession*, pp. 96 f.

427 Lief, *Social and Economic Views of Mr. Justice Brandeis*, pp. 376 f.

428 Fraenkel, *The Curse of Bigness*, pp. 38 f.

429 Lief, *Brandeis: The Personal History of an American Ideal*, p. 319.

430 Frankfurter, *Mr. Justice Brandeis*, p. 104.

431 *Idem, Ibid.*, p. 97.

432 Lief, *Social and Economic Views of Mr. Justice Brandeis*, p. 103.

433 Frankfurter, *Mr. Justice Brandeis*, p. 103.

434 Goldman, *Brandeis on Zionism*, p. 102.

435 Brandeis, *Letter to Alfred Brandeis*, February 18, 1925. In Flexner, *Mr. Justice Brandeis and the University of Louisville*, p. 7.

436 *Idem, Letter to Fanny Brandeis*, October 20, 1924. In Flexner, *Mr. Justice Brandeis and the University of Louisville*, pp. 16 f.

437 Fraenkel, *The Curse of Bigness*, p. 39.

438 Mason, *The Brandeis Way*, p. 174.

439 Fraenkel, *The Curse of Bigness*, p. 72.

440 Mason, *A Free Man's Life*, p. 432.

441 Lief, *Social and Economic Views of Mr. Justice Brandeis*, pp. 381 f.

442 Mason, *The Brandeis Way*, p. 71.

443 Brandeis, *Business—A Profession*, p. 17.

444 In a conversation with me.

445 Lief, *Social and Economic Views of Mr. Justice Brandeis*, p. 147.

446 Fraenkel, *The Curse of Bigness*, p. 46.

447 Lief, *Social and Economic Views of Mr. Justice Brandeis*, p. 226.

448 Mason, *A Free Man's Life*, p. 530.

449 In a conversation with me.

450 Lief, *Social and Economic Views of Mr. Justice Brandeis*, p. 277.

451 *Idem, Brandeis: The Personal History of an American Ideal*, p. 256.

452 *Idem, Social and Economic Views of Mr. Justice Brandeis*, p. 344.

453 Goldman, *Brandeis on Zionism*, pp. 24 f.

454 In a conversation with me.

455 Goldman, *Brandeis on Zionism*, p. 28.